PARABLES
OF
SIVANANDA

PARABLES OF SIVANANDA

Sri Swami Sivananda

Published by
THE DIVINE LIFE SOCIETY
P.O. SHIVANANDANAGAR—249 192
Distt. Tehri-Garhwal, Uttarakhand, Himalayas, India

Price] 2009 [Rs. 55/-

First Edition:	1955
Second Edition:	1983
Third Edition:	1993
Fourth Edition:	2004
Fifth Edition:	2009

[1,000 Copies]

©The Divine Life Trust Society

ISBN 81-7052-037-1
ES111

Published by Swami Padmanabhananda for
The Divine Life Society, Shivanandanagar, and
printed by him at the Yoga-Vedanta Forest Academy
Press, P.O. Shivanandanagar, Distt. Tehri-Garhwal,
Uttarakhand, Himalayas, India

SRI SWAMI SIVANANDA

Born on the 8th September, 1887, in the illustrious family of Sage Appayya Dikshitar and several other renowned saints and savants, Sri Swami Sivananda had a natural flair for a life devoted to the study and practice of Vedanta. Added to this was an inborn eagerness to serve all and an innate feeling of unity with all mankind.

His passion for service drew him to the medical career; and soon he gravitated to where he thought that his service was most needed. Malaya claimed him. He had earlier been editing a health journal and wrote extensively on health problems. He discovered that people needed right knowledge most of all; dissemination of that knowledge he espoused as his own mission.

It was divine dispensation and the blessing of God upon mankind that the doctor of body and mind renounced his career and took to a life of renunciation to qualify for ministering to the soul of man. He settled down at Rishikesh in 1924, practised intense austerities and shone as a great Yogi, saint, sage and Jivanmukta.

In 1932 Swami Sivananda started the Sivanandashram. In 1936 was born The Divine Life Society. In 1948 the Yoga-Vedanta Forest Academy was organised. Dissemination of spiritual knowledge and training of people in Yoga and Vedanta were their aim and object. In 1950 Swamiji undertook a lightning tour of India and Ceylon. In 1953 Swamiji convened a 'World Parliament of Religions'. Swamiji is the author of over 300 volumes and has disciples all over the world, belonging to all nationalities, religions and creeds. To read Swamiji's works is to drink at the Fountain of Wisdom Supreme. On 14th July, 1963 Swamiji entered Mahasamadhi.

PUBLISHERS' NOTE

Truth is simple. Simple are the words of a God-realised saint. How simply our Gurudev, Sri Swami Sivanandaji Maharaj, states the subtlest of spiritual truths, so that even laymen can understand! The Sage's compassion is such that he wants the truths of the scriptures to be made available to all, to whatever intellectual level they may belong. Therefore, he has literally exhausted all the methods of stating the truth. He has written commentaries on ancient texts; he has presented learned theses on metaphysical questions; he has narrated them in the form of interesting stories; he has given laconic expression to them in aphorisms; he has vividly dramatised them in his plays; he has sung them in songs and woven them into sublime poems; and now comes another potent method of instruction—the Parable. The story is interesting; the mind readily grasps it. The spiritual truth which is the other side of the story automatically gets inerasably lodged in the mind. The truth becomes not only clear, but indelible.

These Parables are of incalculable benefit not only for the Sadhaka to meditate upon, but for the spiritual propagandist—with the parables he can drive his sermon home into the heart of the audience.

—*THE DIVINE LIFE SOCIETY*

BHAKTI COMMANDMENTS

1. Develop devotion through *Japa, Kirtan, Sattvic* food, worship (*Puja*), etc. Yearn for God-vision. Love Him with all your heart. Remember Him constantly.

2. Keep the company of saints, the righteous and the wise. Study devotional books like the Gita, the Bhagavata, the Ramayana, the lives of Saints.

3. The Name of the Lord is Divine Nectar. Name is your sole Refuge, Prop and Treasure. Name and *Nami* (God) are one. Always chant His Names with devotion. Do *Kirtan*. This is the principal *Sadhana* in *Kali-Yuga*.

4. Pray to the Lord from the core of your heart: "I am Thine. All is Thine. Thy Will be done. I am an instrument in Thy Hands. You do everything. You are Just. Grant me faith and devotion."

5. Feel the Presence of God with you. See God in every face. Behold the whole world as the Lord.

6. Practise *Sadachara* (right conduct). Cultivate virtues and eradicate vices. Be good. Be kind to all. Be humble. Be pure. Speak the truth. Control anger. Have a large heart. Develop compassion.

7. Teach the eye to behold the Form of the Lord. Teach the ear to hear the Lord's *Lilas* and Glory. Teach the hands to serve the saints and the poor.

8. Take refuge in the Lord. Do total, ungrudging self-surrender. Live for Him. Offer your actions to Him. His Grace will descend on you.

9. Have perfect trust in God. Faith is necessary to attain God. Faith can take you to the inner chambers of the Lord.

10. Constantly repeat some inspiring verses (praises of God's Glory) or some Mantras, or the Names of God. This will be your Divine background of thought.

GLORY OF RAMA NAMA

1. Glories of Rama *Nama* are innumerable.

2. Rama who is All-pervading is realised when the devotee of Sri Rama annihilates egoism, and when all attachments due to egoism disappear by Rama *Smarana* (remembrance at all times).

3. Sri Rama resides in the heart of all individual souls.

4. Rama loves His devotee when he has surrendered his individual self at the feet of Rama.

5. In divine love the devotee is blessed by all-pervading Lord Rama with Self-Bliss.

6. The devotee is always at the feet (at the mercy) of Rama.

7. Rama loves His lover, and thus the devotee is initiated into Rama *Nama* by Rama Himself.

8. The devotee is full of Self-Bliss, and does not feel the necessity of any more than what is acquired through right endeavour by the Grace of Rama.

9. Sri Rama's devotee is directly under the shelter of Rama, and feels joy in the prayer: "O my Lord Rama; ever live in my heart and bless Thy humble devotee with Thy Love only."

10. The devotee finds Rama in all individual souls, and in Divine Love is directed by Rama, and

blessed with patience '*Jo tudh bhawe sai bhali kar, to sada salamat nirankar*'. Thus peace is eternally achived.

11. Rama's devotee is always at the Feet of Rama, and works under the order and Will of Rama. The devotee of Rama works in his own self, belonging to Rama. The devotee devotes his self solely to the Feet of Rama.

12. May All-pervading Rama bless all humanity with Divine Love!

CONTENTS

Publishers' Note	6
Bhakti Commandments	7
Glory of Ram Nam	9

Part One
PHILOSOPHY AND TEACHINGS

CHAPTER ONE: PHILOSOPHY

Parable of the Butter Hidden in the Milk.	19
Parable of the Crow on the House-top	20
Parable of the King's Dream	21
Parable of the Woman Who Wanted to Adorn Her Reflection	23
Parable of the Jack-fruit in the Courtyard	24
Parable of the Man and His Dog	27
Parable of the Zamindar and His Agent	28
Parable of the Lost Wristwatch	30
Parable of the Doormat	31
Parable of the Camel's Satisfactions	32
Parable of the Passenger and His Luggage . .	33
Parable of the Man Who Lost His Mind	34
Parable of the Greedy Pilgrim	36

CHAPTER TWO: THE SUPREME PURPOSE OF HUMAN BIRTH

Parable of the Boy Who Watered the Root . . .	37
Parable of the Pandit and the Shawl	38
Parable of the Cat in the Hammock	38
Parable of the Prostitute and Her Lover	39
Parable of the Jalataranga Player and His Cup	42
Parable of the Koshakara Bird	43
Parable of the Man Who Was Afraid of Mosquitoes	43
Parable of Two Businessmen	44
Parable of the Two Birds and Garuda	46

CHAPTER THREE: THE GLORY OF THE GURU

Parable of the Blind Leading the Blind	48
Parable of the Cunning Man and Four Fools . .	49
Parable of the Millionaire's Messenger	50
Parable of the Pseudo-Bhakta	51
Parable of the Brahmanishtha and His Disciple .	53
Parable of the Good-natured Youth and the Beautiful Girl	55
Parable of the Well-cooked Feast	56
Parable of the Suspicious Man Who Got Drowned	58
Parable of the Luxurious Man	59

Parable of the TB Patient	60
Parable of the Deluded Pilgrim	62
Parable of the Sheep and the Wolf	63

CHAPTER FOUR: THE SADHAKA'S EQUIPMENT

Parable of the Mourning Bird	65
Parable of the Professional Bargainer.	66
Parable of the Gardener and the Shepherd . . .	67
Parable of Jaggery God's Naivedya.	68
Parable of the Patient Poor Man	69
Parable of a King and His Hawk.	73
Parable of the King and the Astrologer	75
Parable of the Bearded Man and Gruel	76
Parable of the Heiress Who Marries the Ugly Man	77
Parable of the Snake and the Rat	78
Parable of the Woman Who Advertised Her Connubial Experiences	81
Parable of the Bigoted Devotee	82

CHAPTER FIVE: THE PATH OF SERVICE

Parable of the Elephant's Bath	83
Parable of the Mother's Trick	.84
Parable of the Boy Who Purchased One Brinjal for One Rupee	84
Parable of the Honey and the Creeper	86

Parable of the Ghee-dyspeptic	88
Parable of the Man Who Washed Mud with Mud	89
Parable of the Two Travellers	90
Parable of the Zamindar's Palace	91

CHAPTER SIX: THE PATH OF GOD-LOVE

Parable of the Tailor's Needle	93
Parable of the Ant and the Lizard	94
Parable of the Inveterate Old Man	95
Parable of the Dacoit	96
Parable of the Blessed Mouse	97
Parable of the Millionaire and Three Beggars	98
Parable of the Wood-cutter and Lord Yama	100
Parable of the Brainy Boy	101
Parable of the Nobleman's Charity	102

CHAPTER SEVEN: CONQUEST OF MIND

Parable of the Ants and Mountain of Sugar	104
Parable of the Girl Who Stopped the Policeman and the Thief	105
Parable of the Poor Man and His Treasure-trove	106
Parable of the Weeds in the Field	107
Parable of the Cheating Postmaster	108
Parable of the Man Who Cut the Cow's Udder	110
Parable of the Advocate's Turban	111

Parable of a Hundred Children	112

CHAPTER EIGHT: THE PATH OF THE WISE

Parable of the Grain and the Hay	114
Parable of Four Learned Scholars	115
Parable of the Boy and the Candle	116
Parable of the People Who Died of Fear	117

CHAPTER NINE: THE NATURE OF THE JIVANMUKTA

Parable of the Hunter's Dream	119
Parable of the Torch in a Dark Room	120
Parable of the Child and the Shadow	120
Parable of the Fire's Pollution	121
Parable of the Cows and the Scratching Pillar .	123

Part Two
OTHER PARABLES

Parable of Raja Janaka and the Pandits	127
Parable of the Old Lady and the Needle	128
Parable of the Mother-in-law and the Beggar . .	128
Parable of the Young Man's Boon	129
Parable of the Sadhu and the Sword	133
Parable of the Boy Who Could Not Tell the Time	135
Parable of the Bird and the Cotton-fruit	136
Parable of the Man in the Python's Mouth	136

Parable of the Boy and the Angel	137
Parable of Water and Fire	138
Parable of the Opium-smokers and Moon's Reflection	140
Parable of the Husband and the Wife	141
Parable of the Pet Child	143
Parable of the Man and His Mud-horse	144
Parable of the Philosopher and the Broken Mirror	145
Parable of the Brahmin Who Escaped Rain	147
Parable of the Conductor Who Fell Off the Bus	147
Parable of the Manager Who Removed the Hands of the Clock	149
Parable of the Boy and His Shoes	149
Parable of the Masked Boy and the Mouse	150
Parable of the Children's Quarrel over Mud-houses	151
Parable of the Man Who Pretended to Be a Woman at the Booking Office	152
Parable of the Bullock-cart Driver	153
Parable of the Puranjana Maharaja	154
Parable of the Unwary Deer	158
Parable of the Laconic Spartan	159
Parable of Mahmud and Ayaz	160
Parable of "The Dramatic Show"	161

PARABLES OF SIVANANDA

PART ONE
PHILOSOPHY AND TEACHINGS

CHAPTER ONE

PHILOSOPHY

PARABLE OF THE BUTTER HIDDEN IN THE MILK

The young daughter had gone to her village home for the first time from her city-dwelling. At night before retiring to bed, her mother opened a pot in which there was good cow's milk and poured a little buttermilk. The girl asked her mother: "Mother, that was butter milk; and why have you mixed it with Milk? The milk may be spoiled!" "Child," answered the mother, "that is the way to prepare the milk in order that we might get butter out of it." "But where is butter in it, mother?" "It is in every drop of the milk, dear; but you can't see it now. I will show you in the morning." In the morning the daughter saw that what was liquid the night before had become solid overnight. Mother put a churning rod into it and started churning the curd vigorously. Butter began to float on the surface of the curd. Then she gathered it all up and presented it to the astonishment of the daughter. The mother explained: "The addition of the buttermilk curdles the milk. Milk is transformed into curd. Then you have to churn it. By this process the butter which was all-pervasively hidden in the milk is obtained. At first you were not able to see it; it was hidden. From where has it come now? From the milk only. Therefore you understand now that it was there all the time. It awaited the process of churning to reveal itself to your great joy." The daughter, too, followed the same process and got the butter, for herself.

Similarly, a worldly man approaches a Mahatma and asks him: "O Sadhu, why have you renounced the world, and poured this new element of Vairagya and Tyaga into your life? Why don't you let the life take its natural course?" The Sadhu replies: "Brother, I do so in order to realise God." "Where is God?" "He is all-pervading." The worldly man does not see and is not convinced. The Sadhu then explains how the inner personality which is fickle and outflowing should be made solid and firm. Then the churning rod of one-pointed concentration and meditation should be taken hold of, and this solid Antahkarana should be very well churned. Then God is realised. He is all-pervading, in every atom of creation. But He is not visible to the naked eye nor is He realisable by a man except through this process called Sadhana.

Just as a mother was necessary for her daughter to learn that butter exists in milk and that churning will bring it out, even so a Guru is necessary for a man to know that God is, that He is all-pervading, and that He is attained through Sadhana. If the aspirant follows the Guru's instructions, he too, can realise God.

PARABLE OF THE CROW ON THE HOUSE-TOP

A man came to a village and asked another man standing at the crossroads: "Friend, which is the house of Mr. Iyer?" "See that house on the top of which a crow is sitting. That is the house of Mr. Iyer," replied the second man. The first one went away. He returned after a week and was bewildered to find that no crow was sitting on the top of any house. Again he asked a bystander: "Which is the house of Mr. Iyer?" He replied: "That house with three storeys, which is built of stones—that is Mr. Iyer's house." Since then he never had any confusion about the house indicated.

Sastras speak of God or Brahman as the Supreme Origin of the universe: "*Yato va imani bhutani jayante*", etc. But this is not enough. For, there are times when there is no creation at all. Hence this is not a permanent definition of Brahman. Therefore they give Eternal Indications like "*Satyam jnanam anantam brahma*", etc. By following these indications no one can ever miss to attain the Goal, viz., Brahman or God.

PARABLE OF THE KING'S DREAM

A king went to bed in his palace, which was guarded on all sides by sentries. Not even a fly could enter it and disturb the king. The bedroom was equipped with every kind of comfort and there was nothing lacking, which enabled the monarch to enjoy the bliss of deep sleep.

Soon after he lay down he had a dream. A jackal had somehow entered the palace, attacked him and had bitten a toe of his left foot. In the meantime he hears the news that enemies have entered his kingdom and took possession of all things. He flees in fear; but the toe gives him great pain. He runs to a doctor for medical aid. The doctor refuses to treat him as, though he was a king, he had no money to pay for the doctor's fees on the spot, for he had lost his kingdom. As a mendicant he runs away to the forest. There he finds a Mahatma who heals the wounds. Gratitude to the Mahatma wells up in the heart of the ruler, when he wakes up.

The dream vanishes. the king is still lying on his golden bed in the palace which not even a fly could enter. He finds that there is neither the jackal, nor the wound nor his running away to the forest. But the Mahatma's grace endures in his mind, and he, though it was all a dream and he has realised it, for ever cherishes the memory of the holy man's healing service and derives inspiration from it.

Similarly, the Jiva is truly the Supreme Monarch of the Universe. There is nothing lacking in it and it is in possession of supreme bliss—it is bliss itself. Yet, when the veil of ignorance is thrown over it, it dreams. In that dream the jackal of egoism bites it. The enemies of the senses overpower it. The happiness that it so long enjoyed is gone; it experiences pain and misery. It runs here and there in search of relief from misery and in search of happiness. Everyone in the world is selfish. Unless there is immediate benefit from it, no one is prepared to give even a cup of water. Disgusted with the ways of the world, it runs to the forest—to the lotus-feet of the Sat-Guru. The Guru heals its wounds and awakens its higher soul-consciousness. The awakened soul perceives everything that happened as nothing but a long dream. Gratitude to the Sat-Guru who healed the Jiva of the dire malady of birth-and-death, alone remains. The Guru's Upadesa and his Grace alone endure when all else that was part of the dream vanishes. The awakened soul once again feels that it is the Supreme Monarch of the Universe, that nothing ever happened to its majesty, that there was no ignorance and no egoism, and that from eternity to eternity it continues to be the self-same Self—all-blissful, peaceful and immortal.

PARABLE OF THE WOMAN WHO WANTED TO ADORN HER REFLECTION

A woman looked at herself in the mirror. Her bare body and head were unattractive. The reflection disgusted her. She ran in and brought a number of ornaments. She began to adorn the reflection with them. But she could not. Then she took the ornament near the image in the mirror, it looked as though (in the mirror) the ornaments are being taken away from the reflection. At last, she started wearing the ornaments on her own self. To her wonder, the image in the mirror also put the ornaments on, and looked beautiful.

The reflection represents the Jiva and the woman the Self or God. The ignorant man finds that he lacks prosperity, wealth and happiness. He hunts for the things of the world and goes on accumulating around himself the wealth and luxuries of the world. These do not satisfy him or enrich his soul! The more he tries to adorn himself with the riches of the world, the farther they seem to recede from him in truth. Then he understands that his little self is but the reflection of the All-Pervading Atman, the Supreme Self. He offers all his wealth to the Self, by doing charity to the poor, by self-abnegation and self-dedication. He serves the poor, the sick and the suffering and brings happiness to them with the Bhava that he serves the All-Pervading Self in all. He offers himself to the Self through meditation on It. He pays no more attention to the little reflection, the Jiva; but devotes himself to the adorning of the Reality. Instantly he finds that he (the Jiva) is the centre of all auspiciousness, of all beauty, of all happiness and bliss.

O man, abandon self-seeking, and seek the Self. You are not this body, mind, intellect and little 'I'; you are the Immortal, All-Pervading Satchidananda Atman. Realise this and be free.

PARABLE OF THE JACK-FRUIT IN THE COURTYARD

A big jack-tree in a man's courtyard was laden with fruits. From the very bottom of the trunk upto the topmost branch it was dotted with fruits. As though one possessed with an evil spirit, the man rushes out towards the fruit several times. He touches the jack-fruit, but the surface is uninviting. He abandons it in disgust. Far away from home he had seen one palm tree. Walking in the hot sun several miles, he stands near the tree. His craving had reached its zenith. The few small fruits that hung on the top of the tree tempt him. He rushes forward. He falls on the bush of prickly pears and gets injured by the thorns all over the body. Not discouraged by this he tries to climb the tree. The scales that cover the trunk are hard and knife-like. They hurt him. But he does not mind. As he climbs, a swarm of poisonous ants that sting like devils, sting him all over the body. He has somehow managed to reach the top; such is his mad passion for the little fruits. The fruits are surrounded by hundreds of bees. When he lays his hands upon them, the bees angrily sting him. In spite of this, he tries to grab the fruits. Then and there he drops more than half the catch. With the remainder, he tries to climb down. Several fruits drop off his hand before he reaches the ground. He sits himself down to enjoy the few fruits left with him. To his horror he discovers that the major portion of these little fruits is hard nut; and then even the skin has to be thrown away. There is little pulp in the fruit. In disgust he throws the fruits away. Instantly he comes back to his senses, and begins to suffer with agony. The pain of the thorns, the bites of the poisonous ants, the stings of the bees, and the cuts produced on his body by the sharp scales of the tree—these seem to torment him all at once. It is now past several days since he left home. With his tattered clothes and bleeding body, he runs home....to find that his father had been waiting for him with the delicious jack-fruit. The young man stumbles into the house and falls at the father's feet. Without asking a question, the father gives him new clothes, pulls out the thorns from his body, dresses up the wounds, all the time feeding him with the honey-like jack-fruit. The young man's happiness is now complete. Peacefully he sleeps on his father's lap.

Similarly, man ignores the fountain of Eternal Bliss that is within the core of his own heart. He is frightened away by the apparent initial difficulties in Sadhana. He does not care to cut open this rough exterior and enjoy the highest bliss. He is hungry. He runs away from home and from this tree that yields the best fruit. Over the burning sands of Samsara he runs hither and thither. Here he falls into the thorny bush of dishonour; there he knocks against the rock of failure. He falls in love with a woman. How many sacrifices—of a care-free life, of freedom from worry and anxiety—he has to make before he approaches her! Lured by illusory pleasure he succumbs to passion.

As he tries to go up this tree of wedded life, a thousand worries about feeding the children, finding money for his wife's sarees and jewels bite him all over the body. Even then he pursues the evil goal. He is intent on the little fruit of sensual pleasure. As he grabs it, several fell diseases prey upon him. He becomes sick of it all and, writhing with pain and disease, he realises that the world would not allow him to enjoy even the little pleasure which he thought was within his grip. He looks for a way-out.

While ascending this tree of family life, and even while descending, the sharp knife-edges of the demands of creditors and relatives tear his clothes and bruise him all over. He is now left with tattered clothes and a body which has been bled at a hundred places, and depleted of all energy. Tired, he sits down for a while and examines the fruits that have caused him all the trouble. Much of it is hard nut (the impenetrable heart of a woman, that gives her love the magic of magnitude, without the least real substance in it!) and part of it is mere skin. When these two are thrown away, there is practically nothing left—except the cuts and bruises, the stings and bites, the torn clothes and tired body. With supreme disgust, the man throws away the illusory fruit and runs home.

There the Guru is waiting for him, with the delicious fruit of wisdom, all cut and ready to serve. He wipes his tears, heals his wounds and supplies the new clothes of renunciation and devotion. The young man falls at the Guru's feet, and rests securely on his lap. With the supreme love and compassion that can flow only from a Guru's heart, the Guru feeds the disciple with the sweet honey of wisdom, of Atma-Jnana. Awakened in his innermost Self, man sleeps to the affairs of the world and enjoys the great sleepless Sleep of Samadhi.

PARABLE OF THE MAN AND HIS DOG

A man went out for a walk with his lovely dog. He was very proud of the dog. It always went before him. This man had an umbrella in his hand. To show the people around him that his pet-dog would do anything for him, he made the dog carry the umbrella between its teeth. And it proudly walked before him, with the middle of the umbrella firmly caught in its teeth. Suddenly it began to rain. The man wanted to make use of the umbrella. But the dog was a hundred yards ahead of him. He ran towards it. The dog, not knowing why the master ran after it unusually, was frightened and ran towards the house at top-speed. The proud man was drenched to the skin, before he could reach the house and recover the umbrella.

The Jiva, blinded by pride and ignorance, entrusts its spiritual consciousness to the mind. For some time the mind seems to walk before and lead the Jiva; and the consciousness is there firmly held by the mind and the Jiva feels that it is safe. There is a heavy shower of miseries of mundane life and temptations of sense-objects. The dog-mind with the umbrella of spiritual consciousness had parted from the Jiva and is separated by great distance.

If the umbrella of spiritual consciousness had not been entrusted to the mind (which incidentally, could not make real use of it), the Jiva could have protected itself from the rain of miseries and temptations. Now, the faster he runs forward to get relief from miseries and temptations, the farther this relief seems to recede.

Thus, O Man, commit not the folly of entrusting thy spiritual wealth and welfare to the defective mind. It is most undependable. It will desert you in the time of trials. Learn to trust in the Lord alone. Make Him thy sole support.

PARABLE OF THE ZAMINDAR AND HIS AGENT

A big zamindar appointed an agent over his estates. The agent had been given vast powers over the estate. People were made to obey him and believe that the power to control them, to appoint them and dismiss them vested in the agent. Though the zamindar was watching the agent and his activities from a distance, he made it look as though he was absent. Gradually, the agent grew more haughty and arrogant and began to assume the powers of the zamindar himself! One day a Sadhu came to see the zamindar. The agent sternly rebuked the Sadhu and said: "Where is the zamindar? There is no such person here. I am the all-in-all. Whatever you want, ask from me." The Sadhu who had wonderful powers, at once shouted out, "O zamindar, please come and enlighten this man!" The zamindar, as though he was waiting for the call, rushed in. The agent hung his head down in shame and fell prostrate at the feet of the zamindar and the Sadhu. The zamindar promptly suspended the agent and reappointed him only when he had thoroughly realised his mistake and had sincerely vowed never to deny the suzerainty of the zamindar, but to sing his glory to all that came in contact with him (the agent).

The zamindar is the Supreme Lord. The agent is the mind. The mind is born of the Supreme Lord; it shines in His light only, and has no independent existence, in truth. But it appears as though its powers are unlimited, because the Self has appointed the mind as Its agent to carry on the Lila of the world. The mind imagines that it is the controller of the senses, that it can give power to or withdraw power from the senses. Gradually, the wicked mind begins to deny a power superior to itself. Then comes the God-realised saint who reminds the mind of the Self. But the wicked man denies the existence of the Self. "Where is the Self or God? I am the all." But the Guru or the God-realised saint is not to be defeated so easily. He shouts the

Lord's Name in the man's ears, and gives initiation. At once the man realises a higher Power.

He recognises the all-pervading, ever-present nature of the Lord. He surrenders himself to the Lord. The Lord at once dismisses the mind. When the mind vanishes, the Sadhaka enters into Samadhi and enjoys the Beatific vision. Then, when he returns from Samadhi, he is a thoroughly changed and chastened man. He vows never more to deny Him, but to sing His glory always.

PARABLE OF THE LOST WRIST-WATCH

A man was frantically searching for something in a dark room. He was weeping and shouting. He was making a mess of the things kept in the room. He broke some and tumbled on others. Yet, what he was searching for he could not get.

A friend came to the threshold and asked for the reason of the man's misery. He replied: "O my friend, I have lost my wrist-watch. It is gone."

The friend said: "How can it go away from here? But, what a fool you are to search for it in the darkness! I have brought the light. Now, calm yourself. Think deeply and try to remember where it ought to be. You will soon discover it."

The man did so, and got the wrist-watch. The friend explained: "The watch was not lost, nor have you gained it now. It was there all the time. But because of the darkness that prevailed in the room, and because you were searching for it where it was not, you did not get it. You were ignorant of its whereabouts. Now that the ignorance is removed, you think you have got it. It was ever yours and was never lost."

Similarly, within the deepest recesses of man's heart is the Self, full of bliss and peace. But blinded by the darkness of ignorance man is unable to see it and experience the bliss and the peace. Searching for happiness and peace, he wanders about among the objects of this world, makes a mess of himself and the things of the world, causes misery to others and to himself, weeps and shouts. But the object of his quest is not found. At last the Guru appears with the lamp of wisdom in his hand. He says to the man: "Remove the darkness of your ignorance with this lamp of wisdom; calm yourself; restrain all the mental modifications. Then analyse all experience and meditate on the result. You will discover the Self. You had not lost it before; nor have you gained it now. It has always been there. Only you were ignorant of it. Now that in your pure heart and calm mind, the Self shines, self-luminous, you feel that you have regained it. In fact you had never lost it."

PARABLE OF THE DOOR-MAT

A man was hurriedly entering the neighbour's house. He found at the threshold a colourful door-mat with the word 'Welcome' written on it. With callous ease he stepped on it with a proud stride. The door-mat slipped from its place, and the man fell down on his back, at the same time kicking the door-mat up. It fell down on the reverse side. He cursed the door-mat and the 'Welcome' written on it, and got up. Instantly his eyes alighted upon the door-mat again; but now he found the words: "Danger: Beware" written on it, i.e., on the reverse side of the same door-mat. He understood that it was intended for those who stepped on it carelessly, tempted by the word 'Welcome'.

A man of little intelligence reads in the scriptures '*Maya tatam idam sarvam*', '*Isavasyam idam sarvam*', '*Sarvam khalvidam brahma*', and thinks that there is no need for vigilance, for Vairagya and for Sadhana, as everything is pervaded by God! He slips down; he has a terrible downfall. Now, how could God thus let him down? Are the scriptures that said "*Maya tatam idam sarvam* (All this is pervaded by Me)" false? No. He looks at them again. Now he discovers another utterance of the Lord: "*Anityam asukham lokam imam prapya bhajasva mam*" (Having come to this world of impermanence and misery, worship Me). Now he realises that if a man is careless and has no Vairagya, he would find that he slips at every step; that though the world is pervaded by the Lord, one should walk carefully and be equipped with vigilance and Vairagya.

PARABLE OF THE CAMEL'S SATISFACTIONS

A merchant had to cross a desert. He engaged a camel to carry his heavy luggage. He loaded all the luggage on to the camel's back; and put a small empty tin also. The camel was breaking under this load and was unwilling to move. The merchant now removed the empty tin and threw it down. The camel felt that the load on his back had been greatly decreased and started to go, crossing the burning sands of the desert, without any further discontent.

This world—this desert of Samsara—is a place where Maya carries on her business. She throws the poor Jiva into the desert with its burning sands of endless pains and sufferings. The Jiva is loaded with countless cares, worries and anxieties, innumerable pains, diseases and sufferings. Occasionally, Maya removes a petty misery from the back of the Jiva; and a little pleasure is thus given to the Jiva. The Jiva foolishly imagines that it has been completely freed from all the miseries of the world and rushes headlong into the desert of Samsara. Poor deluded soul! The load is all the time there on it. It has been deluded by Maya's trick.

PARABLE OF THE PASSENGER AND HIS LUGGAGE

A villager had never before travelled in a train. He received an urgent telegram from his wife living in another distant village that she was very sick and that she wished to see and speak to him. The villager ran to the railway station and purchased the ticket. He got into the train and the train started. Unfortunately, the track just beyond the station was under repairs, and so the train moved very slowly over it. The villager had seen how the train usually sped along. He could not understand why it crawled at such slow speed. He was impatient to reach the wife's village. He began thinking hard and at last discovered: "What a fool I am! I am not only a burden to the train, but I have kept my bedding and trunk also as an additional burden over the train. It is only because of this load that the train is going slow." At once he lifted the trunk and bedding and placed it upon his head — to the amusement of co-passengers.

Similarly, man boards this train of life on earth. He is himself borne by some unseen power. But his wife (happiness) is in grave peril and he wishes to reach her quickly. Things do not always happen here as one wishes them to. The impatient man feels that if he takes on the responsibility of his family and children, of his business affairs and domestic concerns, on his own head, he would reach his destination—happiness—sooner. He forgets or is ignorant of the fact that in any case it is the train that carries him and all the weight that he might put either over his own head or down on the floor of the compartment. God is the protector of all. Yet the foolish man thinks that he is responsible for his wife and children, for his house, business and property.

PARABLE OF THE MAN WHO LOST HIS MIND

A man was playing cricket. Suddenly the ball hit him on the back of his head. His head reeled. Everything went dark. He fell down in a deathly swoon. He was removed to the hospital. After undergoing various operations and injections, he was brought back to consciousness. He asked for something to eat. He cried looking with great fright upon the things around him. He began to question the people around him "Who are you?" "What is this?" The nurses realised that he had lost his mind. He had forgotten all his relatives; he was not able to tell whose son he was. The elderly nurse who brought him back to consciousness played the part of his mother. She adopted him as her son. The man believed that she was his real mother. He cultivated new friendships and made new friends. Hardly a year had elapsed before he was irresistibly drawn to the cricket field again. He played as well as he used to previously, though he could not recognise any of his old playmates. People marvelled at this strange transformation of the young man.

Even so does man play the game of life on this earth-plane. Death seizes him. Everything turns black around him. He loses consciousness. Messengers from the other world take him away; and cut him and torture him for the various sins he has committed while on earth. His consciousness is slowly revived on the earth-plane once again when a mother gives birth to him. He cries at the very sight of the strange things around him. He instinctively takes to his mother's breast and sucks milk. As he grows more and more conscious of the world, he begins questioning: "Who is this? What is this?" He has forgotten his real father and mother—God. The lady who gave him birth here says: "I am your mother." He accepts her as such. Then he develops a new set of relatives and friends. But very soon he begins to play the same old game of life, as he used to, irresistibly drawn by the previous life's Samskaras. Wise men marvel at this mystery of transmigration. Though the memory of his past birth is lost, the Samskaras and Vasanas are not lost! They lead him onward.

PARABLE OF THE GREEDY PILGRIM

A man wishing to go on a pilgrimage took a loan of Rs. 100 from his friend. He went to various places and then returned to his native place. When he met the friend from whom he borrowed the money, and when the latter demanded the amount, the pilgrim asked: "How much should I pay?" "Why, Rs. 100!" "Oh, you want the whole of it back?" What a wonderful question!

Equally wonder is the human being's conduct. The Jiva entered the vast field of Samsara and roamed about in various regions—as a mineral, as a plant, as an animal, and then as a man—with the help of the consciousness borrowed from God. In the human birth, the Jiva once again came very near the Home, viz., God. Now that the journey is nearly over, God demands that the borrowed consciousness be entirely given back to Him. In other words, man should realise that his entire soul belongs to God; and thus, his heart should be offered in its entirety to God. But foolish man, filled with lust and greed, with Moha and attachment, is reluctant to do so. What a great wonder! How powerful is Maya!

CHAPTER TWO

THE SUPREME PURPOSE OF HUMAN BIRTH

PARABLE OF THE BOY WHO WATERED THE ROOT

A father wanted to test the intelligence of his two sons. He allotted each of them the task of looking after a mango tree, promising to reward the boy whose tree yielded the best fruit in abundance. The foolish boy discovered that the leaves were withering off and that flowers were coming up at the end of the branches. Promptly he went up the tree and carefully watered every leaf. The leaves withered still more and the tree eventually died. The wise boy, on the other hand, went on watering the root; the tree was green and healthy and yielded delicious fruits in abundance.

Similarly, God gives human birth to man in order to test the evolution of his intelligence. The foolish man, eager to get the reward of Eternal Peace and Immortality, seeks to pay attention to the satisfaction of his sense-cravings, and to the acquisition of worldly knowledge, for he thinks that it is the right way. He dies the miserable death of an ignorant man. The wise man, on the contrary, devotes himself to the contemplation of God, the Root of all Creation, and thus obtains all the wealth and knowledge of the universe. God is well pleased with him and bestows upon him the reward of Immortality and Eternal Bliss.

PARABLE OF THE PANDIT AND THE SHAWL

A Raja presented a rich Kashmiri shawl to a foolish Pandit. The Pandit had no idea of the value of the shawl. He at once wiped his nose and feet with the shawl. Irate at such stupidity, the Raja ordered that the shawl be taken away from the Pandit who did not know how to use it. And his peon snatched it away from the Pandit.

Similarly, this precious human birth has been bestowed upon us as a great gift by God. But the foolish man wastes it on woman, gold and fame. Death soon comes and snatches away this gift of God, grossly misused by man.

O man, utilise this precious human birth in Japa, study of scriptures, selfless service and meditation. Realise the Self and be free.

PARABLE OF THE CAT IN THE HAMMOCK

The man heard the soft, shrill noise of a baby crying, in the adjoining room. He thought that his baby-son had been disturbed in his sleep. He went to the room and found that there was movement in the hammock. He started singing a lullaby and rocking the hammock. This went on for nearly ten minutes, when, to his amazement, a cat jumped out of the hammock and ran away. Within the hammock he saw that the cat had nicely punctured the baby's feeding-bottle and emptied

THE SUPREME PURPOSE OF HUMAN BIRTH 39

the milk that was in it (The mother had taken the baby out).

Into the foolish man's ears fall the sweet, soft words of endearment that his wife and children utter. He is highly pleased and engages himself in serving them. This goes on for a considerable time, before he discovers that it was not their love for him that made them behave sweetly towards him, but their own selfishness. Inside the hammock of the household which he is managing, he does not find the child of people really devoted to him, but the cat of selfish relatives, who had throughout been busy emptying the milk of his own life and giving out joyous exclamations at having found such a fool as he is!

Brother, look into the hammock. The cat will jump out of the hammock. Do not be duped. Mind your business—the practice of Sadhana to attain Self-realisation.

PARABLE OF THE PROSTITUTE AND HER LOVER

A man was highly infatuated with a prostitute. He would spend hardly an hour at his own house even to take the delicious food prepared by his devoted wife. He never even looked at his wife, and in course of time almost forgot he had a wife, except at food-time. He had a very good friend and well-wisher who, realising that the man was heading towards great misery, took him aside one day and said: "Friend, you know how much I love you. Therefore, I request you to desist from visiting the prostitute." "Why? She is so nice to me and so beautiful. She is my very life. I can think of no enjoyment without her, and no life without her enjoyment." The friend said again: "I have a very good reason for asking you to give her up. You closely examine her body in the manner which I tell you. You will discover that she has got a fell disease. Contact with her will only make you succumb to this disease. Therefore, give her up." The man at once ran to the prostitute and examined her as instructed by the friend. He found out that the friend was correct. At that very moment great disgust for the prostitute entered his mind. He ran away from her house never even to pass by the street in which she lived. His wife was waiting for him in his house. She gave him untainted joy throughout his life-time. Later, even if, due to the force of previous habit, the man happened to pass by the street in which the prostitute lived, she herself would bolt the door and run inside, lest he should, in his anger towards her, abuse her and make it known to her other customers that she has the fell disease. The man, thereafter, constantly enjoyed the edifying company of his wife and enjoyed pure happiness.

Similar is the case of man's transformation. There is infinite bliss in his own heart. But he does not even care to look at this Self; he does not even know that It is there! All the time he is devoted to Maya, the objects of sense-enjoyments. Just for a little while—during deep sleep—he returns to his inner Self and there enjoys peace and happiness; but even then he does not even look at the Self, he does not realise that It is there. His eyes are blinded by ignorance. Now a Self-realised sage comes to him as his dearest friend and benefactor. He says: "O man, give up this Maya; abandon these sense-pleasures. Lo, behold! There is Supreme Bliss within the chambers of your heart. Go there and enjoy Infinite Bliss." But the man retorts: "What foolishness is this! How can there be happiness except in the objects of the senses? I derive the maximum pleasure in the sense-objects. I do not even believe there is any happiness outside these objects. I cannot live without them at all. How can I give them up?" But the sage pleads with the ignorant man: "Friend, look, I have a very good reason for asking you to abandon these sense-objects. They have a great taint. They are perishable and they are tainted with the character of bringing endless misery. Think of disease, think of old age, think of death, these are the qualities of the sense-objects. When you waste your life over them, you get disease, old age and death. Give them up and enjoy immortality and eternal bliss." The man at once sits in a calm place and reflects over the sage's words. He realises the Truth. He banishes sense-objects from his mind. He runs back to his own home—the Seat of the Self—and there enjoys perennial peace and eternal bliss. Sometimes, on account of the force of previous Samskaras, he might even go very near the same old sense-objects. But Maya runs away from him now, lest he should, when tempted by her, expose her nature to others, too, and prevent them from becoming her victims. Thus enjoying the Bliss of the Self throughout his life, he is eventually liberated.

PARABLE OF THE JALATARANGA PLAYER AND HIS CUP

A poor Jalataranga player was enjoying music in his dilapidated house, when it began to rain. Through the leaky roof, water began to drop right on his head. But he was not at all perturbed. Immediately, he took one of the cups which he was so long using to play on, and put it on his head. The cup received the water; and he went on playing as before, till the rain stopped, when he removed the cup from his head, and played on.

The poverty-stricken Jalataranga player can be compared to a young man who is not richly endowed with spiritual Samskaras. The building in which he lives, viz., the body, is not strong enough to resist the forces of nature; energy leaks through its avenues. As a Brahmachari, he studies Vedas and the scriptures in the Gurukula. He is enjoying the intellectual understanding of the great spiritual Truths. But when he becomes a full-fledged youth, there is a heavy downpour of opportunities favourable for the senses to be preyed upon by the forces of nature. He is not led away from the right path. He discovers that among the Sastras that he has been studying there are some which prescribe the Grihasthashram for a young man of his temperament. Thus he gets married. Though it is like carrying the burden of a family, it saves him from greater danger. He continues the music of Sadhana in Grihasthashrama. When the rain of temptations for sensual enjoyment stops, he renounces the world, and then continues the music of Sadhana, without having to carry the burden of the family on his head. He is indeed a wise man.

PARABLE OF THE KOSHAKARA BIRD

The Koshakara bird lives inside the trunk of the tree. It bores a hole along the branch and builds its strong nest close to the bark. In order not to leave any room for invasion by any other creature, the bird goes on strengthening the nest on all sides, and leaves absolutely not a pin-hole in it! If it had left a hole it would get air to breathe. But since it is all blocked, for safety, the bird perishes inside.

Similarly, the Grihastha in his anxiety to shut out misery and pain, builds his nest of home and family, of his internal attitude to life, in such a way as to leave no room for any Vritti other than those of sense-indulgence (the material with which his cage is made), to enter his mind. If he had left one small hole of 'Vairagya' in this shell, he would breathe and be enabled to obtain food for the soul in due time. But, since he does not allow even this, he perishes miserably within this hard and strong nest.

O man, even if you choose to enter the nest of Grihasthashrama, leave a little hole of 'Vairagya' in it, through which you can escape into the Wide World of God-realisation, when the time comes.

PARABLE OF THE MAN
WHO WAS AFRAID OF MOSQUITOES

A resident of a village near a dense Himalayan forest did not get restful sleep in his house. There were countless mosquitoes that literally made a meal of him every night. Disgusted with this, he left the house and began to sleep in the jungle. He did not take the gun; he had no idea of the jungle. The cool breeze kept the mosquitoes away. He was happy. But a couple of days later, a tiger attacked him and killed him.

Similarly, a young man leaves the house, disgusted with its cares, worries and anxieties, and enters an Ashram. But he is not equipped with Sadhana-Chatushtaya, specially Vairagya. For a time, he seems to have attained the object of his quest; for in an Ashram he is not affected by cares, worries and anxieties. But soon, Maya overpowers him and he falls a victim to lust, wealth or fame, and is lost.

PARABLE OF TWO BUSINESSMEN

Two businessmen once set out for a distant land for doing business. They were both rich. They had heard well about the returns that their business would bring them in the new place. The first one, Rama, thought, "Let me invest my entire wealth. Even if the business be shaky in the beginning and there be initial losses, yet my foundation will be strong and I will gain in the long run." Accordingly, he invested his entire fortune and started the business in right earnest, on a well-established ground. With the usual losses in the beginning, he pulled on through the infant stages extraordinarily well and became a well-reputed businessman. As days passed by, he was getting from the establishment more profit than he ever dreamt of.

On the other hand, Govind, the second man, thought with a certain pessimistic attitude: "If I invest all my money and lose it, then I will neither have the profit from the new establishment, nor the fortune to live happily with the old wealth. So let me invest a little at first. If it is profitable, I will invest more and more of the old wealth; for, then, the new profits will help my living and there will not be any need for me to depend on the old wealth for my day-to-day living."

At first, he invested a little. That was consumed by the initial loss account. Then he invested a little, again. It too, was found to compensate only the initial loss without leaving him any profit. As years rolled on, he found that he had lost all his wealth and had nothing to live upon.

The two businessmen are like two spiritual aspirants.

Their going to a far off land is like the aspirants' going into seclusion for reaping a good spiritual harvest.

Like the businessman investing all his wealth at one time, an aspirant renounces his all at once. Like that businessman, the aspirant, too, has got his shaky beginning, but has established himself well in the spiritual path. There is no fall back or final loss. He progresses rapidly and soon attains the bliss of spiritual life, the *summum bonum* of human existence.

Akin to Govind is that aspirant who takes to seclusion foregoing a little comfort, but keeping intact his old fortune to save him in times of need. The aspirant doubts: "If I give out all my wealth and also do not succeed in attaining the Goal, I may be forced afterwards to live like a beggar in this world. So let me keep something in store. On attaining that Bliss, I shall gladly give out this wealth. If I do not attain that bliss, I shall and can utilise this wealth in this world."

This aspirant, like the second businessman, loses all his wealth when Time places its mighty hand upon him. Nor does he get the fruits of spiritual life, like Govind going without profit.

O man! Remember the words of the Lord:

"There is no initial loss here in spiritual effort, nor even reactions. Even a little understanding of this Truth (Law) will save you from very great danger."

Renounce your all, without any reservation; the fruits of spiritual life are there in your hands.

PARABLE OF THE TWO BIRDS AND GARUDA

A beautiful Garuda was flying high up in the skies. Two birds sitting on the ground watched the Garuda soar into the sky and float majestically at an incredible height. The younger bird felt waves of despair rise in its heart. "What is the use of flying at all," it said to the other bird. "If we fly, we should fly like the Garuda. If we can't, it is better to burn away our wings. I am not going to fly at all hereafter." The older bird replied: "Brother, this is not the right attitude. We, too, have wings. And, we can fly. We should not yield to despair. Let us do what we can. There is beauty in that." Saying so, the older bird flew away. The younger one had not got over its dejection, when a hunter came along and easily caught it.

THE SUPREME PURPOSE OF HUMAN BIRTH 47

A saint is ever soaring into the Divine and floating in the transcendental regions of Divine Bliss. All people cannot do that. But everyone has been endowed by God with some good qualities and some talents. Wisdom lies in utilising them as much as you can. If you do not, you are likely to fall a prey to Tamas and sink lower in the ocean of Samsara.

CHAPTER THREE

THE GLORY OF THE GURU

PARABLE OF THE BLIND LEADING THE BLIND

Fifty blind men were sitting in a Dharmashala. They were born-blind. They all wanted to go to a distant place of pilgrimage. Four other blind men came along and joined this group. They said they were also going to the same place. "Friends," said the leader of the fifty, "we are blind and cannot find our way to the sacred shrine. Will you be able to lead us? Do your eyes see?" "Yes, my dear friends," replied the four, "we have heard a lot about the sacred city and the way to reach it. We have a clear mental picture of the route. Though we do not see it with our eyes, we are confident that we shall not only reach our destination, but lead you all there with us. Follow us." They tied one another with a long rope. The best one among the four led the way. He had a mental idea of the way, no doubt; it was not of much avail. He was misled. Soon he fell into a deep ravine. Bound to him, the other blind men, not knowing where he was leading them, also fell into the ditch, one by one. All of them perished.

Similar is the case with the masses today. They hear of the Land of perennial Bliss, the Land where Holiness and Divinity abound. But they know not the way. They are waiting to be led there. In the meantime a few other blind men arrive there. They have heard a lot about the Kingdom of God. They have great intellectual understanding. They think they know the way, and not only that, they can lead others also. They are the scientists and scientific philosophers. They promise to lead the masses to the Kingdom of Immortal Bliss. The credulous public follow them. These leaders have a great intellect, but no self-control and experience. They go where their cravings and Vasanas and desires lead them. They fall into a terrible ditch of sensuousness, of materialism, and perish. All their followers also perish.

Hearken ye, all men; follow not the blind misleaders. Follow the sages who have the eye of intuition and attain the Abode of Supreme Bliss.

PARABLE OF THE CUNNING MAN AND FOUR FOOLS

A man went into a park. All the cement benches were occupied. He was tired and wanted a little rest. None of the occupants of the benches seemed inclined to vacate them. He thought of the best plan. He moved towards the corner of the park and started looking up, pretending to be wonderstruck at the sight. Thus he created eagerness in the four people, occupying the nearest bench, to see what astonished him. Drawn by the curiosity, they left the bench and came near him. As soon as they were near him, he turned round and went straight to the bench and stretched himself on it comfortably. Before they could find out what it was that he saw he had settled down to a nice sleep. The four fools argued for a long time as to what he saw, but could not come to the correct conclusion.

This is what happens to many people in the world. Frequently a scientist or a politician springs up. He wants to lead a comfortable life, with a good name and fame, power and position. He is intelligent; he finds that the common man is a fool who could be easily deceived. This scientist or politician pretends that he has discovered something astounding. People gather around him and worry themselves over his discovery. They enter into endless controversies among themselves over the nature of his discovery; while he himself settles himself down with a fat bank account, roaring fame, all comforts and conveniences.

O fool, be not deceived by the pretender. Approach the sage of true wisdom. He will enlighten you and lead you to the goal, Eternal Bliss and Perennial Peace.

PARABLE OF THE MILLIONAIRE'S MESSENGER

A millionaire wanted to send an urgent message to another rich man living in a neighbouring town. He called his best clerk and handed him the message saying: "Please take this urgently to my friend." The messenger delivers the message to the other rich man. This haughty rich man accepts the message and indifferently tells the messenger: "I hope you have had your food; if you haven't, take this fruit and get away." The messenger was deeply hurt. He goes away. A poor man on the way meets the messenger and with great love and solicitude offers a glass of cool water. The messenger is greatly pleased and refreshes himself with the water. The messenger reports the whole matter to the master who, realising that the insult heaped upon his messenger was verily insult to his own person, looks with disfavour upon the rich man who thenceforward lives estranged from the millionaire. The poor man is amply rewarded.

Similarly, God sends mankind His Messengers in the form of saints and sages. They come to the earth with the message of hope, of joy, of immortality. The haughty man filled with the pride of wealth, position and power, builds an Ashram for the saint or donates lakhs of rupees for the saint's mission;—but all these tainted by arrogance, Ahamkara and Abhimana. This does not please the saint. A poor man, on the other hand offers the saint a flower, a fruit or just water; and with it, he offers his heart to the saint. The saint is well pleased with him. Through the saint, the Lord knows the comparative merits of the rich man and the poor one. He punishes the arrogant rich man and rewards the devout poor man. What matters is Bhava, the feeling; quality, not quantity.

PARABLE OF THE PSEUDO-BHAKTA

Once there lived a coward who had a great desire to present himself before the eyes of the public as a great devotee of Lord Narasimha. He had neither courage nor wisdom, neither devotion nor sincerity. He went to a tattooer to get tattooed on his back the figure of Lord Narasimha. Thereby he thought that people would take him for a staunch devotee.

The tattooer began his work calmly. Within a couple of minutes, the coward, unable to bear the pin-pricks, and obsessed by the fearful thought that a lively Narasimha is coming to sit on his back, tremblingly asked, "Which portion of the Lord are you tattooing?" The tattooer replied that he was just beginning with the legs. The coward said, "Sir, the leg of the Lord gives very much pain. Pray, I don't want His legs. Please tattoo some other part of the Lord." The tattooer again started with the hands of the Lord and the coward replied in the same old way. Then the tattooer began with the head and when he announced it, the very thought of Lord Narasimha's head made the coward tremble violently, and he at once ran away crying aloud, "Lord Narasimha has been pleased with me. He has taken his seat on my back. Look, O men. Look, how great a devotee I am." The people saw on his back a few awkward scratchings made by the tattooer and mocked at the coward, and pitied his folly and ignorance.

The world is full of pseudo-Jnanins, pseudo-Vedantins, pseudo-Yogins. These persons are cowards, but they want to pose for great Yogins and Bhaktas. They do not possess the will to submit themselves to a Guru and learn patiently what the Guru teaches. They cannot face the obstacles in the spiritual path. They just catch a word or two that comes from the Guru's mouth and go about preaching the public under the impression that they have become realised persons. They are just like the coward who thought that Lord Narasimha has taken His abode on his back.

THE GLORY OF THE GURU

O man! Submit yourself whole-heartedly to a Guru. He will write a full ineffable picture of the Lord in your mind. Even without your exhibiting it the public will come to know about the worth of that painting. Bear in mind that you shall have to face the obstacles and overcome them.

Be bold. Be courageous. Be patient. Be earnest.

PARABLE OF THE BRAHMANISHTHA AND HIS DISCIPLE

Once upon a time there lived a certain Brahmanishtha Guru. He was fully immersed in enlightening all humanity with his intuitive knowledge and experience, through all possible means, through delivering sermons, writing books, giving counsels, etc. He employed a certain disciple of his to take down notes, and compile the books. In course of time, the disciple virtually became a gramophone record, always repeating the words and expressions of the Guru. In so doing, he was puffed up with vanity and pride. He went about telling, "What does the Guru know? I remember by heart so many things. I can quote all the scriptures. I am a full-fledged Jnani who knows everything." In short, he became a renegade.

At one time, one of the Guru's devotees was bereaved of a family member. The Guru pitched upon that renegade-disciple and asked him to condole for the bereaved family. The disciple duly went to the bereaved family and began in right earnest to deliver a Vedantic sermon. It all looked like a deaf man referring to cross-purposes. The inmates of the house were still putting on a sad face. All of a sudden, the Guru appeared in person before them. His very presence made them cheerful and happy and forget the loss of the member of their family. The Guru spoke but a word or two; and all of them were instantaneously transformed.

Remember the Kenopanishad, "Which one cannot think with the mind; by which the mind is known" etc.

Intellectual and theoretical philosophers live in vain in this world. They are of no use to humanity. Their talks do fall on the ears of the public like the Vedantic sermon given by the disciple to the bereaved family.

Can the moon say that it shines by its own light, that it helps you with its own light, that its light is superior to that of the sun? When the sun rises, the truth of the greatness of moon's light is plainly known.

So too where there is intuitive experience and knowledge, knowledge arising by itself in an experiencing heart, of what use is the knowledge of the brain?

Sages and saints and men of realisation live to enlighten all humanity. Even if they keep quiet, their very presence is able to transform all humanity, whereas a dry intellect cannot enlighten even one individual.

O man! Forget your intellectual attainments. The knowledge that you possess is not yours, but it belongs to the Lord. Acknowledge His superiority and submit to His will.

THE GLORY OF THE GURU

PARABLE OF THE GOOD-NATURED YOUTH AND THE BEAUTIFUL GIRL

There once lived a young handsome youth who was proverbially good to all. He never did an act neither directly or indirectly detrimental to human progress and good. Once he went about on a tour. On his way, he met a beautiful girl and immediately fell in love with her. She, too, did not object to it. Without much delay and deliberations, the young man returned to his house with the girl. But, prior to the date fixed for marriage, the young man learnt all about the girl's love for some other youth, as evinced by her through her actions. Without hesitation, he got her married to that man. A year passed by. The girl was about to forget the kindness of the good-natured youth. The youth, taking the help of a magician gave the girl a certain drug in the form of sweetmeat, on taking which she developed hatred for her husband; and abandoning him, returned to the good-natured youth. Thenceforth, they lived a happy life till the end of their life.

God and Guru are synonymous. They are comparable to the good-natured youth. All things that they do are always for the good of the individual and the universe.

The youth picking the girl is like God or the Guru choosing the disciple from the world.

The girl's love for another man is akin to the devotee's or disciple's love for earthly things. God and Guru allow it in the case of their beloved devotee and disciple. But when the individual is about to forget God or

Guru, they through their mysterious spiritual powers (comparable to the magician's drug) turn the mind of the individual from all earthly objects and take him to their own respective abodes.

Their act of diverting the individual from worldly pursuits is transcendental, unquestionable. But, it is for the great good of the individual.

PARABLE OF THE WELL-COOKED FEAST

Once upon a time there lived a Brahmanishtha Guru with a certain disciple of his. They were both living in one and the same Kutir. The disciple duly studied and mastered the various scriptures. He also served the Guru day and night.

His proximity with the Guru made him think that he was the only beloved disciple of the Guru. This further led him to believe that the other disciples, who were wandering hither and thither all through the year and occasionally visited the Guru, were not truly devoted to the Guru. All that only strengthened his ego.

One wintry night, the disciple returned to the Kutir after finishing some outdoor work. He heard the voice of another disciple, an occasional visitor, inside the Kutir. He knocked at the door. The Guru asked, "Who is that?" The disciple replied, as usual, "It is I, please open the door."

The Guru replied, "I am enjoying a well-cooked feast. There is no room for a second one in my feast."

The disciple misunderstood the Guru. He thought he was belittled and insulted before an occasional visit-

THE GLORY OF THE GURU 57

ing Gurubhai, almost a stranger for all practical purposes. So, being annoyed and offended, he left the place immediately and went about wandering aimlessly.

As days rolled by, his heart, mind and ego got thoroughly burnt by the fire of separation from the Guru. His heart and mind, his very being as well, were cooked well by the fire of Viraha. He forgot himself and went almost mad with Guru-Bhakti.

One day, all of a sudden, he rushed towards the Guru's Kutir and kept on knocking at the door aloud: "Gurudev, Gurudev" in a rich love-ladden tone. That very sound drowned even the Guru's usual and formal question, "Who is that?" His mind was filled with the presence of his Gurudev alone. He was blind to everything, nay, neither he nor the universe existed for him; only the Guru existed.

The Guru knew well the voice of his disciple. He could no longer wait. He, too, rushed out and affectionately embraced the disciple, saying "I am now enjoying a well-cooked feast. There is no room for a second one in my feast."

God is omnipresent and non-dual. There is no room for a second one to exist by Him. There is no room for that little self of man in this vast universe.

As long as the little ego persists, you, too, should be wandering in the dark, undergoing all hardships like the proud disciple. In that state your being religious, your visiting temples and places of worship, your observing austerities—all those things cannot make you the beloved of God.

You should have Ananya-Bhakti, love of God for God's sake. Mere service of God with the thought "I am serving God" cannot become Ananya-Bhakti.

When your ego is consumed by the fire of Viraha, when your heart and mind are well cooked in that fire, nay, when your love for God is well cooked over the fire of separation, and becomes delicious and palatable to Him, when, in that state, neither you nor this universe exist to you, but only He exists filling your heart and mind, then and then alone, will you become the beloved of God. He will then rush towards you and embrace you like the Guru embracing the disciple.

Then both of you will enjoy a well-cooked feast at which there will be no room for a second one.

Kill the little self and say:

"O Lord! All this is Thy Own Self."

PARABLE OF THE SUSPICIOUS MAN WHO GOT DROWNED

Two men are standing on a rock in an ocean, away from the shore. It is getting dark. Clouds are gathering in the sky. Even a sight of the shore is lost. Waves are lashing on the rock. The ocean is getting turbulent.

In that darkness a man appears before them.

"Come with me, I shall take you to the shore," he says.

The wise man readily follows him.

But the fool questions: "How will you take us across the waters?"

"I have got a boat with me," says the new-comer.

"I am ready to come with you," says the wise man.

"No, I won't come," says the fool; "suppose the boat is defective or the man is a dacoit?"

The wise man gets into the boat and safely reaches the shore, guided by the boatman. The fool is quickly swallowed up by the rising waves of the ocean.

Floating along in this ocean of Samsara, the Jiva, after great struggle, gets this boon of a human birth. The other shore of safety has not yet been reached. Time is fleeting. The evening of life has set in. Eye-sight is lost. The eye of wisdom is blinded by the gathering clouds of materialism and disharmony. Perplexed and prayerful the man stands on the rock of individual life.

The Guru comes to him with the boat of the Lord's Name or of Bhakti. He beckons man to follow him and get into the boat, and thus safely cross over to the shore. The wise man readily does so. But the fool has a thousand doubts and a million misgivings. He questions the bona fides of the Guru, and the validity of Bhakti. Very soon he is once again swallowed up in the huge ocean of Samsara; and, sunk in it, he has lost the greatest opportunity of saving himself, given to him by God.

PARABLE OF THE LUXURIOUS MAN

He was very rich. He led a luxurious life. He ate delicious dishes. He would throw away anything which did not come up to his highly developed sense of taste. This high living gave him violent dysentery. The doctor prescribed for him the most bitter pill. "Unless you take this bitter pill, you will die," he said. Without another word, the man took the pill and became well. Once for all he gave up the life of luxury so that he might never again fall sick.

When there is abundance of energy, in the full bloom of youth, man leads a sensuous life. He is accustomed only to the best of everything! He would scoff at renunciation, self-sacrifice, self-denial, etc. He is not interested in anything that does not give him the maximum sensual pleasure.

His physical energy is depleted. The Guru comes to him and points out to him that he is suffering from the most deadly disease of birth and death. He gives him the bitter pill of renunciation, self-sacrifice and self-denial. Because this is the only way of escaping from the disease of birth and death, the man swallows the pill, and resolves at that very moment, never to revert to his old life of luxury, of Godlessness and heedlessness.

PARABLE OF THE TB PATIENT

A man is suffering from tuberculosis. The doctor finds that the disease cannot be got rid of so long as the patient is alive. Yet, he does not want to say so. Very encouragingly, he tells the patient: "Brother, you can be completely cured. But you must realise that the disease is a very serious one. It cannot be cured by medicine alone. You will have to observe strict dietetic restrictions. Then you can easily get rid of the disease." The patient assures the doctor that he would observe the dietetic regulations in strict accordance with his instructions. The doctor gives the medicine. The medicine is only an excuse for imposing the wholesome dietetic regulations on the patient. The patient takes the medicines and observes the dietetic regulations for some time and finds that the disease does not cause positive misery to him. With great joy he continues the treatment. The disease does not leave him altogether; but it does not cause much trouble, either. The disease lies within him, without manifesting itself; and dies with his natural death.

Similarly, when an aspirant approaches a spiritual preceptor, he lays before the preceptor his history, the many sins he has committed and the many evil Samskaras that are within him. The preceptor discovers that all of them spring from the greatest disease of ignorance, Mula-Ajnana, which can be cured only when the body-idea disappears. Yet, the Guru initiates the aspirant into a Mantra and says: "This is a very good medicine; but unless you practise Ahimsa, Satya and Brahmacharya, unless you get up at Brahmamuhurta and meditate, unless you are regular in your Sadhana, it will not be of much use. You must do selfless service, be devoted to God, meditate. Then you will be rid of this inner malady." The aspirant takes to the Mantra and practises the Sadhana. Soon he finds that he has a light heart, a clear mind and a subtle intellect. His conscience is clear. Encouraged by these salutary signs, he continues both the Mantra-Japa and the Sadhana.

The evil Vrittis die by themselves within his Antahkarana, as they have no chance to manifest themselves. If, by God's Grace, he gets spiritual enlightenment before his death, with the death of his body, his Ajnana also dies, and he gets cured of this terrible disease of birth and death.

PARABLE OF THE DELUDED PILGRIM

Thousands of people were arriving at Rishikesh to have a dip in the holy Ganga. One man was rushing into the station and purchasing a ticket for Madras. Astonished that he should leave Rishikesh on such a holy day, without taking the opportunity to bathe in the Ganga, a pilgrim asked the man: "Brother, are you not going to be at Rishikesh on this holy day and take bath in the Ganga? Can you not postpone your visit to the South?" The man replied: "Friend, what is there in Ganga? I have taken bath in the Ganga day-in and day-out for several years. I have heard that he who takes bath in the Tamraparni river in the extreme South of India gets great merit. So, I am proceeding there." The people laughed at his foolishness.

People living with a great saint for a long time, often let their devotion to him wane. While millions of people from all parts of the world come to the saint to have his Darshan, the very disciples of the saint who are near him always feel that their salvation lies in some pilgrimage or in some Sadhana, to practise which they have to leave him! It is a great pity. It is better not to be overfamiliar with saints and always keep the flame of devotion to their lotus-feet bright within you, unless your devotion to them is firmly established.

PARABLE OF THE SHEEP AND THE WOLF

A man was guarding a large herd of sheep. He sat on a small mound and drove away all the wolves that tried to approach the herd, even when the wolves were at a great distance. Evening set in. The man thought within himself: "Throughout the day I could deal beautifully with the wolves; not one could ever come anywhere near the herd. Nothing will happen at night, either. The wolves may not come at all; and even if they come, I will deal with them properly." Night fell. Whenever the wolves howled near the herd, the man would shout and imagine the wolves had run away. But throughout the night, the wolves were busy carrying away several sheep. When the sun rose again, the man discovered that more than half the herd had been taken away from him. He became wiser and even while the sun was shining the next day, he gathered enough fuel and lit a very big torch which drove away the darkness even when the sun had vanished in the western horizon; and in the blazing light of the torch he was able to see clearly and keep the wolves away.

Even so is the case with the Sadhaka. So long as he is in the living presence of the sun of his spiritual preceptor, he is able to guard the sheep of his spiritual Samskaras from being devoured by the wolves of vices. The deluded Sadhaka imagines that as he is able to guard the sheep against the wolves in the presence of the sun of his Guru, he is proof against sin. He feels that sins would not even approach him now! He ventures out. He wanders away from the preceptor, imagining that he is a Jivanmukta. He delivers fiery lectures attacking sin, vicious life, and Maya. But in the darkness of ignorance, made manifest in the absence of the Guru near him, the Sadhaka loses most of his virtues. Silently the wolves of vices, against which he himself has been shouting all the time, enter him and rob him of the greater part of his virtue. Then, when he returns to the Guru (if, by God's Grace, he himself had not been swallowed by the wolves of vice before his returning to the Guru), he discovers that he has lost much of his spiritual wealth by going away from the Guru. Becoming wiser, he now busies himself in acquiring the fuel of Sadhana-Chatushtaya, Yama, Niyama, etc. Even while he is in the living presence of his Guru, he lights up the torch of Discrimination. When this torch is lit darkness does not approach him at all; and the wolves of vices do not trouble him any more. Then is he, really a Yogi and Jivanmukta. The light of the Guru shines for ever in and through him.

CHAPTER FOUR
THE SADHAKA'S EQUIPMENT
PARABLE OF THE MOURNING BIRD

Two birds—one male and the other female—had built a nest on the branches of a tree. They had a small family of young ones. Generally, the male bird would go out in search of food, while the female guarded the young ones. One day, when the male bird was out, a hunter came and aimed at the female bird. Though the female bird saw this, she was unwilling to fly away, lest the hunter should kill the young ones. Finding his opportunity, the hunter brought down the female bird with one arrow. The male bird just then returned to the nest and finding the dead female in the hands of the hunter, began to weep and wail along with the young ones. If, instead of that, it had betaken itself to its wings, it would have escaped alive. But as it sat thus mourning over the death of its mate, the hunter aimed another arrow at it and brought it down, too. Then he had only to climb the tree and collect the young ones. The entire family thus perished without an effort at saving itself.

Such is the case with human beings here. The parents are greatly attached to their children and grandchildren, and do not notice the approaching death; even when death stares them in their face, attachment blinds them and they cling to their children, while death inevitably drags them away. When a dear one dies, it is a signal for the bereaved person to betake himself to his wings of Viveka and Vairagya and fly away to the Realms of the Immortal, by doing rigorous Sadhana. On the contrary, the bereaved one wails over the loss and gets more and more attached to the family. The hunter (death) easily gets the next victim. Thus, one by one, people enter the house of Yama, without offering the least resistance. Even though they know that death is inevitable, they sit idle inviting it, instead of busying themselves in conquering it. O man, you have the wings of Viveka and Vairagya; fly away before the hunter takes you away.

PARABLE OF THE PROFESSIONAL BARGAINER

After taking much toddy, a man went into a milkstall and took some sweets and *pan* (betel leaves). On coming out he extolled the quality of milk sold in that stall, and said in an impressive way, "I have had just now a cup of milk in that shop. See, it has refreshed me and has given me enough strength and energy to come and roar in front of you. You, too, go to that shop and taste that milk."

The *pan* cannot prevent his mouth from giving out the toddy-smell. His actions were not steady and betrayed his state of intoxication. People readily understood that that man has taken not milk but toddy and that he spoke not for guiding others along the proper lines, but to earn a wage, to procure money, for fulfilling his cravings. Therefore the Public condemned him and shunned him.

The bargainer-cum-drunkard is like the religious hypocrite who goes about preaching religion to earn money to satisfy his lower desires. Such people trade upon the religious faith of the public.

These hypocrites first plan well. They go to some spiritual resort for a short stay, like the drunkard going to the milk-stall. They put on external marks to cover their lower nature, like the drunkard chewing *pan*. They, then go about preaching, posing themselves for fully realised sages, and talk about the heavenly bliss that they are enjoying. They talk impressively, but the public do understand their lower nature and cravings. These false preachers are condemned and shunned from every quarter.

O man! your actions betray your thoughts. You cannot pose for that which you are not. Know this, and mould yourself. Become a true spiritual hero, and not a hypocrite.

PARABLE OF THE GARDENER AND THE SHEPHERD

A gardener was proceeding towards his master's house one morning, with a flower-pot on his head; and in the flower-pot was a beautiful, green plant in growing which the gardener had taken immense pains. On the way he met his friend the shepherd who was going to his house with a sheep slung on his shoulders. The gardener had not met the shepherd for some time. He greeted the shepherd with a big smile and the two began to talk. When the exchange of news came to an end, they went their way. The gardener wanted to take a look at the plant, before he entered the master's house. He lowered the pot from his head. To his horror, he discovered that there was not a leaf left in it, and that it was all but a naked stem. The sheep which his friend had around his shoulders had eaten away all the leaves while he was busy talking to him. How could he enter his master's house without the plant? He, therefore, returned to the garden, sorely disappointed.

A Sadhaka cultivates divine virtues in the garden of his heart. He has to struggle hard and exert much in order to cultivate even a single virtue. The virtue is a passport for him to enter his Master's House, the Kingdom of God. He carries the pot of his virtues, as it were, while proceeding to the Kingdom of God. But during his journey of life here, he meets a 'friend', who has with him the eater of virtue, viz., vice. Contact with this friend seems to be amusing to the man of virtue. But this is costly friendship. Very soon, the virtuous man discovers that the company of the 'friend' has denuded him of his virtues. He has lost the passport to the Kingdom of God. He has to return to this world of pain and death, sorely disappointed.

O man, beware of wrong company. Have Satsanga. You will be spiritually elevated.

PARABLE OF JAGGERY GOD'S NAIVEDYA

Having heard of the efficacy of worshipping the image of Vinayaka prepared out of jaggery, a man wanted to perform daily Puja to a jaggery-idol. He was a great miser. He did not want to spend much money on the Puja. Anyhow, he got the idol prepared and commenced the Puja. When the time came for offering Naivedya (food-offering) to the Lord, the miser did not know what to do. He had not brought anything for Naivedya, nor was he willing to purchase anything. He found that the idol had a big belly (Vinayaka is supposed to have had a big belly); and the belly was made of jaggery. "This jaggery itself will do for Naivedya," he thought. With a pen-knife, he cut a small piece of the Vinayaka's belly, placed that jaggery on a plate and offering it to the idol as Naivedya. To teach him a lesson, Vinayaka made him such a pauper that he had to feed on his own flesh and die a miserable death.

Some people approach saints and sages with impious intentions. They have heard that the worship of saints bestows all prosperity and glory on them. They approach the saints and speak honeyed words. They are misers. They will not spend even a pie on charity. They will even go to the extent of deceiving the saints taking flowers and fruits from the saint's own abode and making a show of offering them to him! Even the little prosperity and intelligence they have is taken away from them; and they eventually die a miserable death, sunk in ignorance and delusion.

PARABLE OF THE PATIENT POOR MAN

There was a rich old noble who lived in a great palace. There also lived nearby a poor man in a dilapidated hut, who subsisted on crumbs of food cast away by others. But he was ever cheerful, and never complained of his ill-luck.

Once it so happened that the poor man had nothing to eat for a long while. So he went to the rich noble for help. The old noble received him kindly and asked what for he had come. The poor man said that for days he had nothing to eat and that he would be happy if he was given some food. "Is that all!" said the noble. "Come, sit down!" Then he called-out; "Boy! A very important guest has come to dine with me. Ask the chief to make ready the dinner at once, and bring some water to wash our hands."

The poor man was surprised. He had heard that the noble was a very kind man, but he did not expect such a ready welcome. He was all praise about his host. The noble at once interrupted him and said, "Don't mention it, my friend. Let us sit down for the feast." And the old noble began to rub his hands as if some water was poured on them and asked the poor man why he did not wash his hands.

The poor man found no boy or water but decided that he should do what he was told, and so he pretended to wash his hands likewise. "Now let us sit down to dinner," said the noble, and began to order various delicious dishes. But there was no trace of any food or even a single bearer.

Then the noble said to the poor man, "We have such wonderful feast before us. Enjoy yourself, my friend. You must finish all these fine dishes." And the noble pretended to eat from imaginary plates.

THE SADHAKA'S EQUIPMENT

The poor man was faint with hunger, but kept his wits. He did not allow despair to overcome him. He also pretended to eat from the empty table. The noble now and then exclaimed, "What a delicious soup! The curry is wonderful, isn't it my friend?" The poor man replied, "Sure, sure!" "Then why not have some more," and the noble pretended to dish out some imaginary curry. Likewise, he pressed more and more imaginary dishes on the poor man and asked him if they tasted all right.

Though desperately hungry, the poor man thanked his host profusely and said that he had never eaten such a glorious feast in his life. He did not betray a sign of remorse. He kept on maintaining the face cheerfully without the least affectation, as though everything was real.

The noble was a generous person. He was a man of charitable disposition. He wanted to test whether the poor man would give way to despair. He had heard of his reputation that he never lost patience. He thought that such a contented, cheerful person as this poor man should not starve and suffer from poverty. But he had his doubts. So he himself wanted to test him. Now he found that all that was said about him was true.

The noble then clapped his hands and a retinue of servants came in with all the delicious dishes he had been mentioning. An elaborate dinner was laid on the table. This time the poor man did not have to pretend. He now ate heartily with the noble.

After they had finished their meals, the noble said, "Friend, you are a man of infinite patience. You know well how to make best of everything and bear adversity cheerfully. You are the man I was looking for to manage one of my farms. You should live with me hereafter."

Thereupon the poor man did not have to suffer any more from poverty.

This story has several lessons for the common man to learn. When the poor man went to the rich man, he did not ask for any charity so that he might dispense with begging for some days. This shows that he was not greedy. He lived in the present. He wanted some food and he asked for only that. Now, if he had asked for some money, he would have got it, and would have spent it in a few days, only to revert back to his former poverty. He did not ask any more than what he needed immediately, and this paved the way for his good luck in being employed in the rich man's farm.

When the poor man was harassed by his host with imaginary dishes, he did not lose his patience in spite of his extreme hunger. If he had done so, he would have been asked to get out and would have lost his dinner as well as his unforeseen appointment.

He did not either complain about his ill-luck or bewail his misfortune as an ordinary beggar would have done before a rich man.

Hence the moral is that one must be patient and make the best of everything. One should learn to bear adversity cheerfully, do one's best, pray to God, and trust in His grace. One should never complain about one's misfortune. As one soweth so one reapeth. Hence there is no use in bewailing ill luck. One must

THE SADHAKA'S EQUIPMENT

learn how to master courage and build one's destiny through self-effort.

Patience is golden. Without patience life will be a total failure. One important point in this story is that when one goes to somebody for any favour, one should be prepared to nod to his tune if anything is to be expected from him.

Greed and the grace of God cannot live together. Where there is greed, there good luck can hardly exist. One should learn to live in the present, and ask for nothing more than one's due.

With patience, cheerfulness, contentment and amiable disposition one should learn to make the best of the circumstances one is situated in.

PARABLE OF A KING AND HIS HAWK

A king had trained a hawk for purposes of hunt and reconnoitre. He used to take the hawk with him whenever he went out. Once the king and his huntsmen were riding home through a valley between the desert dunes. The king felt very thirsty. As he rode along the valley he found, to his great joy, some water dribbling down the edge of a rock. He at once dismounted and held out his silver goblet to collect some water. Meanwhile, his pet hawk which he carried with him, flew out and began to circle over the dunes.

After some time, when the cup was full, the king raised it to drink the crystal clear water with great eagerness. But before he could do so, the hawk suddenly swooped down from above and flapped its wing against the cup, so that all the water was spilled.

The king looked up and saw his pet hawk alight upon the top of the rock from where the water trickled down. He picked up the cup and held it again to collect the trickling drops. He had to wait a long time until the cup was full, and then when he was about to drink the water, the hawk dived down as before and knocked out the cup from the king's hand.

The king grew very angry. He collected the water again with great patience and for the third time the hawk did not allow the king to drink it.

The king was furious by now. He drew out his sword and shouted at the hawk: "This is the last time. If you prevent me from drinking the water, you will pay with your life. "He collected the water again patiently, and this time he was wary with his sword as he raised the cup to drink the water. The hawk did come down again and knock out the cup, but as it did so, the king cut off its head with a quick sweep of the sword.

He grunted, "Now you had your lesson!" As he looked down for his cup, he saw that it had fallen inside a crevice where he could not get down. So he began to climb up the rock to drink from the source. When he reached the top he found there a pool of water inside which there was a dead poisonous snake. The king was stupefied. He no longer remembered his thirst but only thought of his hasty action which resulted in the killing of the hawk which saved his life. The king then resolved, "I have learnt a bitter lesson today, i.e., never to do anything in haste."

Haste is the mother of grief. Develop discriminative power. Think well, and then act. Look before you leap.

PARABLE OF THE KING AND THE ASTROLOGER

A king produced his horoscope before an astrologer and asked him about his future. The astrologer pondered the positions of the planets and consulted the Sastras and finally gave his verdict: "Maharaja, all your relatives will die before you, you will perform their obsequies with your own hands." The king became furious. He was very much attached to his relatives and could not tolerate such a verdict. The king at once ordered that the poor astrologer should be given imprisonment for life.

Then the king sent for another astrologer. This man was more tactful than the first. He found that the previous astrologer's readings were absolutely correct. So, he tactfully put the same truth the other way round. He said: "Maharaja, you have a very long life. You will live longer than all your relatives." This also meant that all his relatives would die while the king was alive. The same fact had been very tactfully told to please the king. The king was highly pleased with the astrologer and gave him rich and costly presents.

Therefore it is said that, even while telling the truth, one should tell it in a pleasant manner. Even a truth should not be told in a way that will hurt the feelings of others. If it is told so, it is tantamount to untruth only. Your speech should be truthful, pleasant and beneficial.

PARABLE OF THE BEARDED MAN AND GRUEL

Once a man with long beard and moustache was offered a glass of gruel (paste-like porridge) that will stick to the beard and moustache and spoil both. He liked the gruel so much that he could not afford to lose it. He also liked his beard and moustache which he tended so carefully and lovingly everyday. In his efforts to drink the gruel without spilling it on his moustache or beard, he took great care and exercised much caution in holding the glass at a distance, and the net result was that the entire gruel fell on the ground and nothing went into his mouth.

The bearded man is like a half-baked aspirant. His tending the beard and moustache is akin to the half-baked aspirant's devoting his time to keeping his physical cloak neat and beautiful.

The gruel is the wisdom-nectar that the spiritual teacher offers unto him.

In his efforts to keep the body free from pain, affliction, austerities, etc., the half-baked aspirant tries to keep himself aloof from the practice of Sadhana. He thinks that without doing practical Sadhana, he can derive permanent happiness in life.

Nor can he forgo heeding the instructions of the spiritual teacher, because they promise him the highest good. And the instructions that he receives from the Guru never do him any good, for he wastes them due to his folly. So, too, his stay with the Guru proves to be of no use to him. He has to learn much from experience, and then change his attitude. He has to abandon his love for the body and for bodily comforts, try to be benefited by his proximity to the Guru, by the instructions that he receives from the Guru.

Immortal life is for the Spirit and not for the flesh. You can enjoy the former, only when you transcend the latter.

PARABLE OF THE HEIRESS WHO MARRIES THE UGLY MAN

There once lived a beautiful young heiress to a very great fortune. Many young men sought her hand in marriage. But she preferred to choose an ugly-looking poor youth who became perverted and unsteady in his worldly activities, on account of his love for that young lady. When the other suitors asked her the reason for her selecting a man who had neither good looks, nor wealth nor brain when compared to them, she replied:

"You can never be compared to that poor man; nor do you possess his eyes which are able to see both the worlds."

To be awake in love is hypocrisy.

The young heiress can be compared to the Lord possessing all wealth.

The poor, ugly-looking youth is compared to a devout aspirant who knows not anything beyond the Lord, to whom all the three worlds are verily found within his goal, there being nought besides it.

The other suitors are like devotees who pray for gifts from the Lord, but not for the Lord Himself.

To be awake in love is hypocrisy, for thereby you do not love the beloved for what the beloved is worth independently, but for the beloved's external beauty and riches.

To be awake to the external world is to forget the Spirit. It is worse than sleep.

Whether it is Vedanta or Bhakti or Yoga, it is all the same, as far as the main aim is concerned. You should forget the external world, be blind to it, and see all space and time within your Goal, the inner Reality.

Then the Self will reveal Its nature unto you; then God will love you and choose you as His best devotee.

PARABLE OF THE SNAKE AND THE RAT

A venomous cobra had been caught and put in a basket. It was starving within. Intending to subdue it thoroughly and bring it under his control, the snake-charmer had given it no food at all for several days. The snake-charmer was away. Over the basket a rat was playing. The cobra knew it was the rat. It addressed the rat thus: "O Rat Maharaja! You are so kind and generous. You are indeed the king of all animal kingdom. Kindly shower your grace upon me!" The rat asked: "Who are you, speaking from within the basket? Are you not the cobra, my greatest enemy? Why do you flatter me like that?" "I am not flattering you, the Emperor of emperors," replied the cobra. "I hereby swear that I shall never again touch any rat in my life. Therefore, be gracious towards me." Pleased with the humble attitude of the cobra and the words of praise that it had uttered, the rat said: "O cobra, you are true; I am the Emperor of emperors now, because I am beyond your reach. You are nicely caught in the basket. I am pleased with your words. Now tell me what shall I do for you." The cobra replied: "May my forked tongue ever sing thy glories, Maharaja! I pray that you might make a small hole on the top of the basket. This you can do in a minute; and that is all the favour I crave for." "Pooh!" said the proud rat, "Is it for this small favour that you have been so humbly praying to me? I will do it in a second." The rat instantly set to work. Even before the hole could be completely made, the cobra sprang out of the basket and swallowed the rat first, before escaping from the snake-charmer's dwelling. On the way the cobra met the snake-charmer and bit him hard, so that he, too, died of the poison.

The Snake-charmer is the Sadhaka. The snake is the vicious mind—the lower impure mind full of vicious Samskaras and Vasanas. The basket is the little Tapasya and Sadhana that the Sadhaka does to keep the vicious Samskaras in check. The rat represents just a little bit of good Samskaras formed in the mind which is yet laden with love of luxury and sense-pleasure. The rat thus plays a dual-role.

With great effort the Sadhaka "catches hold" of the vicious mind and puts it in the basket of Tapasya and Sadhana. The vicious Samskaras are starved out, by the Sadhaka's refusing to give them their food in the form of Vishaya-Bhoga. The Sadhaka now feels that by this method he will soon be able to be a full master of the mind and make it do as he wills. But, when he is away, i.e., when he relaxes his vigilance a little bit, an object of worldly pleasure approaches the Sadhaka. The vicious mind rejoices inwardly. It tries to make friendship with the object. But the slightly illumined intellect says: "You wicked mind, you are my sworn enemy; how, then, do you think, I shall release you from this restrictions of self-control? Will I allow you to indulge the senses once again?" The wicked mind is cunning, too. It sings the praises of the object of enjoyment, painting it in divine colours. "You are not a temptation to me at all! Wealth is an instrument for doing service and charity. Women are my divine mothers. Luxury is just the hire that I grant this body which is ceaselessly working for the welfare of humanity. I have vowed never to indulge the senses." All hypocritical words!

It vows never to sin, never to indulge the senses, though released from the restrictions of self-control. A hole is made in self-control; there is a channel for the partially controlled mind to flow out towards the sense-objects. The vicious mind first makes a good meal of the little Viveka that has dawned in the Sadhaka, before it enjoys the sense-objects. Then while escaping—and the natural vicious force of the mind is redoubled now, on account of the starvation of the senses, and the repression of the desires—the vicious mind goes headlong and kills the Sadhaka. The Sadhaka perishes because of the lack of vigilance, and because of the small hole made in his Sadhana, in his Tapasya, by the contact of the lower mind with sense-objects.

O aspirant! Beware. Beware. Beware. Slacken not your efforts, your Sadhana, or your Tapasya, even for a second. Stick to your resolves. March to your Goal.

PARABLE OF THE WOMAN WHO ADVERTISED HER CONNUBIAL EXPERIENCES

Modest women never tell others the sweet words of love whispered into their ears by their fond husbands, nor of their connubial experiences. A foolish woman thought, in her extreme pride of her husband's love, that if she told others how dearly her husband loved her and illustrated this with the words he had uttered in her ears and the happiness she has derived from his company, people would admire her and congratulate her on her good fortune. When she began broadcasting these experiences of hers, people laughed at her and mocked her and her own relations avoided the company of this immodest woman. Eventually, even the husband began to hate the wife for such immodest behaviours on her part. Thus she lost everything and spent the rest of her life in utter misery.

Similarly, good Sadhakas never tell others of their Guru's Upadesa or their spiritual experiences. But foolish Sadhakas, proud of their initial spiritual experiences, begin to advertise them in order to draw public attention and admiration. But, alas, the public discover his vanity; and he becomes the laughing stock of the people. Brother-Sadhakas shun his company as he is a man of vanity. Overweaning pride makes him lose even the initial contact with the Divine that he had and thus he forfeits the spiritual experiences granted to him. Thus abandoned by all, he spends the rest of his life in utter misery.

O Sadhaka! Keep your Guru's Sacred Upadesa and your spiritual experiences a secret. Then you will grow spiritually and reach the goal quickly.

PARABLE OF THE BIGOTED DEVOTEE

A foolish devotee had a golden image of Buddha, which she took with her wherever she went. In the course of her wanderings, she came to a monastery where hundreds of images of Buddha were present. She did not like the other Buddhas, she liked only her own. Whenever she burnt incense before her Buddha, she never liked that the fumes should go to the others. She drew a curtain round the image. In a few months her Buddha became dark and grim, while the others were shining brighter, still.

Similar is the case with the narrow-hearted persons. They do not honour others' faith. But as a river without tributaries suffers dearth, their faith too lacks firmness and dies an immature death. One should develop the heart to embrace the other faiths, also. The religion that embraces all and fights with none is the real religion. Such a religion alone will endure, while others will vanish like bubbles. such an enduring religion is the religion of truth, purity, non-violence and love.

CHAPTER FIVE

THE PATH OF SERVICE

PARABLE OF THE ELEPHANT'S BATH

A Mahout took an elephant to the Ganga and gave it a nice bath for over an hour. He applied pounds of soap and scrubbed its whole body nicely. He was thoroughly satisfied. He took it out of the water and was driving it home. The moment the elephant reached the bank of the Ganga, it took with its trunk a large quantity of dust and dirt and smeared its whole body with it. The Mahout realised that all his effort was wasted upon it. He drove it back to the forest and made it lift logs of wood. He extracted much work from it. Whatever effort he put forth in this direction was not wasted at all! He realised that the elephant was fit only for this, and it was wiser to take work from it than to waste time in bathing it.

Elephant is a Tamasic being. A Tamasic man given to all kinds of vices is comparable to the elephant. The Mahout is a saintly soul. The saint tries to clean the vicious man with the soap of scriptural knowledge and bathes him with Japa, Kirtan, etc. But the moment he finds a chance, the vicious man sprinkles dust and dirt upon himself. The saint understands the vicious man's nature. He puts him to hard work. He extracts much useful work from him. The vicious man works like the elephant. Work eventually purifies him.

PARABLE OF THE MOTHER'S TRICK

A mother was trying to give an ounce of bitter medicine to her child. However much she might caress and cajole the child, he would not take the medicine. She hit upon a wonderful idea. She placed a sweet 'laddu' before the child and said: "If you take this medicine, I will give you the laddu." At once the child drank the medicine. As the medicine removed the effect of the disease and gave him abundant energy, he ran away in great joy, even forgetting the 'laddu'.

If you tell a man, "Please do this Yajna (sacrifice)", he will not do it, because he seeks pleasure through every action. Therefore, the Vedas offer Svarga, etc., as rewards for sacrifices. When man performs the sacrifices, his heart is purified and gradually wisdom dawns in him. He does not even bother any more about Svarga and the finite happiness there. In Supreme Bliss he gets liberated.

PARABLE OF THE BOY WHO PURCHASED ONE BRINJAL FOR THE RUPEE

A man had two sons. He gave them ten rupees each one day and said to them: "These ten rupees you can spend as you like. But please bring me some brinjals for tonight's dinner."

They both went away to the bazaar. The foolish boy produced the ten-rupee note to the vegetable seller and said: "Please give me ten brinjals for the whole amount; my father wants to give a good dinner tonight."

THE PATH OF SERVICE

The vegetable-seller at once noticed the foolishness of the boy, gave him ten rotten brinjals and sent him away.

The wise boy went to the shop and produced a ten-rupee note and said: "Look, I want ten brinjals—the best ones at the cheapest rate. And, give me the balance." He got the brinjals for four annas. With two rupees he did Puja in the local temple and took the Lord's Prasad. He gave away five rupees in charity to poor boys who heartily blessed him and his family. For the balance he purchased the best spiritual books available in the book-shop.

They both returned to the father and produced what they had brought.

"Look, father what I have brought! Ten brinjals for ten rupees; they ought to be wonderful," said the foolish boy, and produced the ten rotten brinjals. The father threw away the brinjals in great disgust, remarking: "You have not only lost the money, but purchased rotten brinjals which would spoil even other good dishes. What a fool you are!" Turning to the other boy, the father asked: "What have you brought?"

The wise boy lay before the father the good brinjals, the sacred Prasad from the temple, the spiritual books, and added: "Father, these cost me only five rupees. I distributed the other five rupees in charity. How happy the poor boys were! They sent up heart-felt prayers to the Lord to bless us all. Surely, the Lord is well pleased with us all." The father warmly embraced the wise boy and appreciated his wisdom. "You are my own. I am well pleased with you. I hereby make you the sole heir to all that belongs to me. You and I are one."

The Lord gives riches to people in order that they might utilise the same properly. Artha should be utilised in such a way that it satisfies all the three other Purusharthas—Dharma, Kama and Moksha—and not one (viz., Kama) alone.

The foolish man, however, spends all his wealth, all his energy and time, on the enjoyment of sensual pleasures. These pleasures that he purchases at such expense—are they really pleasures? No, they are all pain and rotten at the very core. They are useless.

The wise man, on the contrary, spends sparingly on the necessities of life, and lavishly on those items that enhance Dharma and earn Moksha for him. He does charity, he spends on Puja, etc. He obtains Jnana with the help of his wealth. (He feeds Mahatmas and Sadhus; looks after their bodily comforts, so that they could impart Jnana to him and look after his spiritual progress.)

The Lord is well pleased with the wise man. He embraces him. They become one. The man inherits divine Aisvaryas and shines as His Divine Heir—a great saint, Siddha and Jivanmukta—on earth.

PARABLE OF THE HONEY AND THE CREEPER

There was a big tree in the jungle. On the top of a branch there was a very big honey-comb. But the ascent to the top of the tree was difficult. One had to cut

THE PATH OF SERVICE

steps on the trunk of the tree and ascend; but that demanded great patience and intelligent work.

A slender creeper entwined that tree and reached up to a greater part of the height. It appeared to be strong, though it perilously dangled in the air.

A greedy man, desirous of possessing the honey, without much effort, began to ascend the tree with the sole help of the creeper. He was too lazy to cut steps on the trunk of the tree and thought that the creeper was strong enough to take him to the top. When he was a few feet above the ground, a violent wind broke the creeper and the man fell down and fractured his limbs.

Similar is the case with those who try to ascend the tree of Divinity, in order to drink the honey of Moksha, with the help of the creeper of Kamya-Karmas, like Yaga, etc. The path to Moksha lies along the trunk of the tree of Divinity. You have to improvise steps on it, with some effort, which is Sadhana. You have to ascend step by step, starting with Yama, Niyama, Asana, Pranayama, Pratyahara, Dharana, Dhyana and then the pinnacle of Samadhi. There is no short-cut to this. You cannot evade this responsibility. If, on the other hand, you climb with the help of Kamya-Karmas—though they, too, appear to be strong—they will not take you to the heights of Atmic splendour. When the wind of selfish desires, greed for the things of this world and the pleasures of heaven, blows, this creeper of Karma will break, and you will have a terrible fall.

O man, selfish works will not lead you to the Goal of Self-realisation. Only unselfish works will help you.

Sadhana means something much sterner. You have to ascend to the top through the hard way. But once you reached the top, you will drink the nectar of Immortality and Eternal Bliss.

PARABLE OF THE GHEE-DYSPEPTIC

A man took too much of ghee during a feast. He became ill. His digestive functions had become paralysed. He went to a doctor. The doctor said to him: "Please bring me one tola of ghee; I will prepare the medicine and give you."

The sick man was wonderstruck; "O doctor, I am suffering only from the effects of too much of ghee-drinking. Why do you wish to add to the trouble?"

"My dear man, please bring the ghee. I will show you what to do with it. The same ghee is your medicine now."

The sick man brought the ghee. The doctor added a few other ingredients to it and administered it in the proper dose. The man was cured. His appetite returned to him.

Similarly, by Karma is man bound to this wheel of birth and death. Egoistic action done with desire for fruits brings about rebirth with all its attendant miseries. The man approaches a saint for a cure. The saint prescribes service, work or Karma again! Can work itself snap the bonds of work? Yes. If the ingredients of selflessness and egolessness are added to it; and if it is done, not for the purpose of securing rewards here or hereafter, but for the purpose of curing one of the dire disease of birth and death. Then it becomes Nishkama-Seva that will release man from this cage of Samsara.

PARABLE OF THE MAN WHO WASHED MUD WITH MUD

A young man had heard it said: "*Ushnam ushnena shamyati.*" One day he was walking along the road, when he found he had to cross a muddy canal. On reaching the other side of the canal, he found that his feet were covered with mud up to the knee. He at once began to apply more mud, up to the waist. A wise man passing by asked the young man what he was doing. He replied: "I am trying to remove the mud." "But you are adding to it!" "That is in accordance with the rule that like cures like." "O fool," said the wise man, "that rule does not apply to this. By adding dirt to dirt, you will only become more dirty. Remove the mud by washing it with water and soap." The young man did so, and was clean.

Similarly, the Jiva which is thrown into this pool of mud, called Samsara, revels in it and adds more mud to it by performing all kinds of Kamya-Karmas (actions with desire). It is led to believe that through such actions it will reap a rich harvest of happiness. But, as a matter of fact, the result is just the reverse. The Jiva is bound more and more strongly to the wheel of birth and death by these chords of Avidya, Kama and Karma. The Guru comes and enlightens the Jiva. He says: "O man, this is not the way to attain eternal bliss or salvation. Wash the dirt of Karma that has given you this birth here, with the water of Bhakti to God, and with the soap of desirelessness. Spiritualise all your actions. Then will the dirt that has covered your soul be washed away and you will shine in your pristine glory." The disciple thereupon practises Bhakti and Nishkama-Seva, and is finally liberated.

PARABLE OF THE TWO TRAVELLERS

Two men were travelling along a village road. One man gave out a cry, caught hold of his foot and sat down. He was in pain. A big thorn had entered his foot. He was unable even to lift it. The other man went ahead and then began shouting at the former: "You fool, it is getting late. If you don't come running, we shall not reach the destination before nightfall." The other man replied: "No, my friend; I cannot move an inch forward till this thorn is removed." "Why are you making such fuss on the way? Come on, get up; or, I will go away," and the friend went a furlong farther. He too had trodden over a thorn and writhing in pain sat down. As even a touch aggravated the pain, they were not able to remove the thorns themselves. There they were suffering the same agony, but separated from each other by unkindness; unable to help each other! Till a third traveller came along and removed the thorns from their foot, they lay down there. The third man came and removed the thorns and said to them: "Friends, they jest at scars that never felt a wound. If you had removed the thorn in the other man, when he had one in his foot, he would have accompanied you, and when you had the thorn in your foot, he would have helped you. Thus would you march rapidly towards the goal, not by ignoring each other's pain."

Similarly, a hard-hearted man, when he finds a fellow-traveller on this thorny and rugged path called life, stricken with pain and penury, laughs at him and goes his way. The nature of life itself is such that he, too, is soon stricken by the same kind of pain and penury. Beyond the reach of all help, this hard-hearted man also suffers. There comes a sage of supreme wisdom, who has the consciousness of Unity, and relieves them of their misery, and in the hearts of both implants the seed of love. He says: "O man, pain exists in the other man only in order to give you an opportunity to serve him and relieve him of his misery. Thus, serving each other, would you evolve rapidly and proceed to your destination. You may laugh at the other man's misery and say it is his Karma; but soon you might find yourself in the same condition. Understand the nature of the world. Serve all. Love all. Realise the Self in all."

PARABLE OF THE ZAMINDAR'S PALACE

A big zamindar had built a wonderful palace. To exhibit his wealth, he had lavished upon the palace all the costly features of art and architecture that the artists and architects of the time could think of. The palace was completed. It was unrivalled. The opening ceremony was made in all pomp and grandeur. The zamindar had invited many people to this function. Some admired the paintings that adorned the wall. Some admired the frescoes on the walls themselves.

Some admired the superb construction of the halls, others the art lavished on every threshold. Only the engineer who was in charge of the actual construction of the palace remained silent. The zamindar asked him: "Well, friend, why are you silent? What is it that you admire most in this paradise which owes its birth to me and in shaping which you had such a wonderful part to play?"

"Pardon me, Maharaj; I had for a time completely lost the consciousness of the surroundings. While I was contemplating upon the grandeur of the palace, I saw before my mental eye, two sturdy bullocks going round and round the *chuna-mixer* (lime-mixer). I greatly admire their service. All the glory of this magnificent building belongs to them. What would these architects, engineers and artists have done if those two bullocks had not patiently gone round the lime-mixer, toiling at the task of producing the best lime for use in the construction?"

In every grand enterprise there are beautiful things that catch the eye. There are spectacular things that strike awe and wonder into your heart. In the tumult of admiration of these glittering objects, you are apt to forget the silent, unostentatious selfless service rendered by the dynamic workers who have helped you build up the mission. To them belongs the real glory.

CHAPTER SIX

THE PATH OF GOD-LOVE

PARABLE OF THE TAILOR'S NEEDLE

A tailor was at work. He took a piece of cloth and with a pair of shining, costly, scissors, he cut the cloth into various bits. Then he put the pair of scissors at his feet. Then he took a small needle and thread and started to sew the bits of cloth, into a fine shirt. When the spell of sewing was over, he stuck the needle on to his turban. The tailor's son who was watching it asked him: "Father, the scissors are costly and look so beautiful, but you throw them down at your feet. This needle is worth almost nothing; you can get a dozen for an anna. Yet, you place it carefully on your head itself. Is there any reason for this illogical behaviour?"

"Yes, my son. The scissors have their function, no doubt; but they only cut the cloth into bits. The needle, on the contrary, unites the bits and enhances the value of the cloth. Therefore, the needle to me is more precious and valuable. The value of a thing depends on its utility, son, not on its cost-price or appearance."

Similarly, there are two classes of people in the world—those who create dissensions and disharmony, who separate man from man; and those who bring about peace and harmony, who unite people. The former are generally the rich people, powerful politicians and kings; the latter are generally the poor devotees of God, the penniless wandering monks and mendicants. The Lord makes use of both to carry on his function of providing the field for the evolution of individual souls. He throws down on the dust the mighty kings and millionaires who create wars and disharmony; and He keeps the poor, pious devotee over His own head. In His eyes the scale of values is entirely different!

PARABLE OF THE ANT AND THE LIZARD

With a grain of sugar, the ant is enjoying its meal. Two young men are watching the self-forgetful way in which the ant is applying itself to the task. Fast runs a lizard, to devour the ant. At a little distance it halts for a while to take proper aim.

One young man says: "Look, the lizard wants to eat the ant. It is the Law of Nature. It is written in the law that the ant is the lizard's food. Watch."

The other young man says: "No. We should not idly stand by, while the lizard swallows the ant. I will prevent it." Saying so, he tries to catch the lizard with its wagging tail. Lo, a part of the tail is in his hand, but the lizard proceeds unaffected. Instantly he covers the ant with the cupped palm of his hand. Its fury made futile, the lizard discovers that the ant is well protected, and vanishes.

Even so when a Sadhaka tries to meditate, the old Vishaya-vasanas come to swallow his Sadhana-Sakti. While he remains for a while absorbed in the joy that meditation on God gives him, the formidable foe from

THE PATH OF GOD-LOVE 95

within rises to attack. The pessimistic foolish Sadhaka gives up effort, in despair. But, the wise one does not. Often in his underestimation of the power of darkness, he tries to give a straight battle to the enemy. The evil Vritti is not caught thereby, but it escapes his grasp and draws nearer. The light of wisdom dawns in him and he quickly covers the Antahkarana absorbed in meditation with the powerful shield of the Name of the Lord and total self-surrender to Him. Thus shielded by the Omnipotent Name, he remains safe and his meditation proceeds unhampered. The evil Vritti, its power totally lost, vanishes.

Yield not to despair. Wrestle not with evil. Cultivate its opposite virtue. Take refuge in His Divine Omnipotent Name. Taste the Immortal Bliss.

PARABLE OF THE INVETERATE OLD MAN

During his youth this man had earned much wealth, indulged in many vices, and had been a very powerful being. Ripe with age and experience, his body has lost its vigour and he lies on the pial weak and worn-out. But even then his desire is to see that none but his friends enter the house! He is anxious that no religious men should enter his house, lest they should preach another-worldly doctrine which he thinks is not conducive to the material progress of his family. He holds his heavy walking stick and sits at the entrance to the house. No one can pass without being noticed by him. Even though he is unable to see, he would ask everyone who tries to enter the house: "Who are you?" and only his old friends would be allowed! The pious men who had endeavoured to bless the house are even now kept away. In course of time he dies, and then they go into the house, do Bhajans and Sankirtan and convert it into a veritable Vaikuntha.

In the heart of the wicked man, desire is manifest in all its diabolical strength. Repeated knocks and blows in this world, and the depletion of the vital energies, diminish the strength of desire. But even when it is considerably weakened, it sits at the entrance to the Antahkarana and never allows any holy thought to enter the mind. Even when it cannot actively indulge in sensual pleasures, it is unwilling to let the Jiva enjoy Satsanga and Sankirtan. With the big stick of delusion and doubt it drives away all divine influences. But the Lord's Grace descends, and desire dies. The divine influences that were till then waiting for a chance, then crowd round the Jiva and enable it to realise its Divine Nature.

PARABLE OF THE DACOIT

There was very rich millionaire in a small town. One night, as he and his family-members were all asleep, a sound was heard. A very strong and powerful dacoit entered the house through a hole made in the wall. Before his strength, the millionaire and his family could do nothing. The robber mercilessly killed them all and himself took possession of the house and the wealth.

Filled with a thousand kinds of Abhimanas resides the ego in man's heart. A sound is heard. The Lord's

Name is sung by Sadhu and Mahatma, and this man hears. That is all. The greatest dacoit, God, enters through his ears into the heart, and, there, ruthlessly annihilates his egoism and his very big family composed of Kama, Krodha, Lobha, Moha, Mada, Matsarya and all kinds of Abhimanas; and the Lord Himself takes possession of the heart and the mind with its vast riches of talents and intelligence.

PARABLE OF THE BLESSED MOUSE

Close to a mountain-stream there was a dilapidated building full of rat-holes. A great number of rats dwelt in those rat-holes. They went out in search of food at night and they got plenty from the neighbouring grocer's shop. They stored the foodstuffs in the holes and dwelt in apparent peace. The mountain-stream suddenly swelled one day and the flood-waters washed away all the rats dwelling in the holes. They died almost instantaneously and floated along the water. As the water dashed once again in huge waves and washed away yet another rat, on the crest of this wave floated a huge log of wood. A rat somehow managed to scramble upon it. It was borne safely down the turbulent stream, because the log was of immense size. A mile farther down-stream the log was washed ashore; and the rat also was safely deposited on the sandy bank of the river. While the others perished, this blessed rat alone was saved.

The mountain-stream is comparable to this terrible Samsara which is nothing more than the current of Raga-Dvesha. The dilapidated house is this little mud-hill called the earth with only the sky as the roof, broken into several fragments by big oceans, with huge rivers running here and there, somewhere high with mountain-ranges, somewhere low with oceans. In this dilapidated house there dwell human beings in rat-holes called towns, villages and cities. Unconscious of the terrible stream of Raga-Dvesha flowing by, people go about their business of greedily gathering the objects of this world. Being caught in the current, they are washed away by this terrible current of Raga-Dvesha. They perish. But, there floats on this very current the log of wood viz., Bhakti. It seems to be part of the stream; though it looks like Raga (a great liking), it is safe because it is an intense liking for God. The blessed soul quickly stands upon this log of wood, Bhakti. The current does not swallow him. He is not affected by the current of Raga-Dvesha. In course of time, he is taken to the shore of Immortality.

PARABLE OF THE MILLIONAIRE AND THREE BEGGARS

There was a good-natured millionaire in the town. Three beggars thought of approaching him for help. The first man went to the millionaire and said: "O Lord! I want five rupees. Please give me." The millionaire was taken aback at this man's impudence. "What! You demand five rupees from me as though I owe you the money! How dare you? How can I afford to give five rupees to a single beggar? Here, take these two rupees and get away," he said. The man went away with the two rupees. The next beggar went to the millionaire and

THE PATH OF GOD-LOVE

said: "Maharaj! I have not taken a square meal for the past ten days. Please help me." "How much do you want?" asked the millionaire. "Whatever you give me, Maharaj," replied the beggar. "Here, take this ten rupee note. You can have nice food for at least three days." The beggar walked away with the ten-rupee note. The third beggar came. "Maharaj, I have heard about your noble qualities. Therefore, I have come to have your Darshan. Men of such charitable disposition are verily the manifestations of God on earth," he said. "Please sit down," said the millionaire. "You appear to be tired. Please take this food," he said, and offered food to the beggar. "Now please tell me what I can do for you." "Maharaj," replied the beggar; "I merely came to have the Darshan of the noble personage that you are. You have given me this rich food already. What more need I get from you? You have already shown extraordinary kindness towards me. May God bless you!" But the millionaire, struck by the beggar's spirit, begged of the beggar to remain with him, built a decent house for him in his own compound, and looked after him for the rest of his life.

God is like this good millionaire. Three classes of people approach Him, with three different desires and prayers. There is the greedy man full of vanity, full of arrogance, full of desires. He demands the objects of worldly enjoyment from God. Since this man, whatever be his vile desires, has had the good sense to approach God, He grants him some part of the desired objects (even these very soon pass away, even as the two rupees the first beggar got are spent before nightfall).

The other type of devotee prays to the Lord for relief from the sufferings of the world, but is better than the first one, inasmuch as he is ready to abide by His Will. To him the Lord grants full relief from suffering, and bestows on him much wealth and property. The third type is the Jnani; he knows the nature of God. He merely prays to the Lord: "O Lord, Thou art Satchidananda; Thou art Existence-Absolute, Knowledge-Absolute, Bliss-Absolute, etc., etc." What does he want? Nothing. But the Lord is highly pleased with his spirit of renunciation, of desirelessness and of self-surrender. Therefore, He makes him eat His own food, i.e., He grants this man Supreme Devotion to Himself. Over and above this, He makes the Bhakta live in His own House—Vaikuntha. For ever afterwards this Jnani-Bhakta dwells in the Lord's Abode as a Liberated Sage.

PARABLE OF THE WOOD-CUTTER AND LORD YAMA

One day, in the month of June, when the sun was at its highest, an old wood-cutter was labouring at the task of collecting a bundle of wood. He was heaving sighs and dragging his weary steps upon the burning path. Being thus exhausted he threw the burden on the ground and prayed to the God of death: "O Death! Please do come, take me away, and relieve me of this burden." And lo! the God of death came to him at once, to relieve him of the drudgery of his mundane existence.

"I have come," he said, "be prepared to meet me."

THE PATH OF GOD-LOVE

"No, No," he retorted, "I did not call you for that. Please keep this burden on my head. Only for this I called you here. Kindly help me to lift this burden." The old man thus resumed his journey tottering with the load on his head.

People of the world, too, generally evince great devotion to the Lord, and pray to Him for relieving them of all the miseries of the world. But their devotion is half-hearted. They never mean what they pray for. They rather prefer to continue their miserable existence here than be relieved of it altogether.

For quick spiritual progress one must develop an intense aspiration to meet God. Suppose your hairs have caught fire; with what rapidity will you rush to quench it? The same must be your eagerness to run to Guru or to God, for attaining liberation. Who can see the Lord? He who cannot live without Him even for a second.

PARABLE OF THE BRAINY BOY

A devotee was distributing the Lord's sacred Prasad outside a temple. Hundreds had gathered around him. They created much noise and confusion. No Prasad could be distributed. A small boy saw this crowd and ran into his house. He brought a big stick to the end of which he had attached a small basket. Standing away from the crowd with the help of the long stick, he took the basket very near the devotee. The devotee admired the boy's intelligence and immediately gave him a lot of Prasad. The crowd that had gathered was still fighting to get near the devotee to receive the Prasad!

The Lord has with Him infinite Grace to be showered over all mankind. But people rush here and there, and want to get to the forefront. Even Sadhakas and devotees who crowd round temples and Ashrams aspire for position and rank! In the meantime, a simple child-like man, with a high degree of Viveka, approaches the Lord with the help of the long stick of meditation and basket of Bhakti. Living away from the maddening crowds, this Bhakta reaches the lotus-feet of the Lord first; because of his meditation and his devotion. The Lord is well pleased with his Viveka, his eagerness to avoid the crowd and reach a first place amongst them; and He is pleased with his meditation and devotion and grants him Divine Grace quickly.

PARABLE OF THE NOBLEMAN'S CHARITY

There was a millionaire in a small town who was far-famed for the magnanimity of his heart. People used to compare him with Karna of the Mahabharata, who never refused anything to anybody. One day a poor Brahmin approached him for help. The Brahmin narrated the millionaire all his difficulties and pleaded for help. The rich man said: "I will certainly do what I can to help you," and sent the Brahmin away. Soon after, the millionaire sent the Brahmin plenty of gold, rice and other provisions, silk clothes and furniture. The poor Brahmin was beside himself with joy. He never expected so much. He only expected Rs. 5. But he got things worth over a thousand rupees. But to the rich man, that was nothing. He even felt that the poor Brahmin might not be satisfied with what he gave. So he had the things sent to the Brahmin; and the Brahmin was doubly grateful for this, too. "Without even giving me the trouble of carrying all this, the noble man has sent them through his own servants," he thought with supreme gratitude. He entered the millionaire's service and served him throughout his life.

The millionaire is God; and the poor Brahmin is a pious Sadhaka. Troubled on all sides by innumerable desires and cravings, the Sadhaka resorts to the lotus-feet of the Lord, for relief from them. Through prayer and meditation, he approaches the Lord. He feels His divine Presence within him. He receives the assurance from the Lord that His Grace will descend on him. Lo, behold! The flood of Grace very soon washes out all the Trishnas and Vasanas and fills the Sadhaka's Antahkarana with the golden virtues, food-grains of knowledge, clothing of Vairagya and the other items of Sadhana-Chatushtaya, and the furniture (sofa, chair, etc., intended to sit comfortably and relax himself) of meditation and Samadhi. To the Almighty these are nothing, for He can even confer Indrahood and Bramanhood on his devotees! But, for the Sadhaka they mean something invaluable. The Sadhaka is thrilled to feel that the Lord did not even wait till he had departed from this world and gone to His Abode, but had sent His gifts to the Sadhaka's own abode—this world. Filled with supreme devotion, the Sadhaka ever afterwards serves the Lord and dedicates himself to the dissemination of His Glory and His Lilas.

CHAPTER SEVEN

CONQUEST OF MIND

PARABLE OF THE ANTS AND MOUNTAIN OF SUGAR

There were thousands of ants living on a hill of salt. Being informed by an ant that there is a mountain of sugar nearby, some ants went to have their fill from it. Many of them walked on and on, but throughout the mountain they could find nothing except salt, because they had in their mouths salt particles which they were reluctant to leave aside. Some few left aside the particles of salt and took their mouthfuls of sugar, thinking that they are carrying the whole of the mountain!

Similar is the case with the ordinary persons of the world, who cannot find Bliss even if they are informed that the mountain of Bliss lies with them, or that they are walking upon the mountain itself, for they are reluctant to leave aside the attachments and selfish ends to which they are fast bound.

Mind itself is the cause of bondage and liberation. If the salt-particles of attachment are not renounced, one cannot get abiding peace anywhere, throughout the universe. Some few are able to practise renunciation to a small extent. Thereby they experience only a little reflection of Bliss. Blessed is he who merges himself into Bliss, thereby becoming Bliss itself, the result of the supreme renunciation of all desires and attachments.

PARABLE OF THE GIRL WHO STOPPED THE POLICEMAN AND THE THIEF

A notorious dacoit was almost caught red-handed by the policeman. With his booty on his hand, the dacoit started running away. The policeman gave him a very good chase. They had hardly run a couple of furlongs before both of them saw a beautiful girl walking alone along the road. The policeman was about to catch the dacoit. But as soon as he looked at the girl, he stood still like a statue. The dacoit, too, was attracted by the girl; and he, too, stood still, a few yards away from the policeman. The girl merely cast a glance at both of them, and walked away. As soon as she was out of sight, the policeman suddenly recollected that he was chasing the dacoit, and the dacoit realised that the policeman was after him. They once again began to run, the policeman chasing the dacoit. But the vigour of the chase is lost; the dacoit escapes.

The vicious lower, impure mind is the dacoit. The higher, pure Sattvic mind is the policeman. The Sadhaka takes a pious resolve to root out the impure Vasanas lurking in him. The higher Sattvic mind begins to purge him of the sinful Vasanas. The chase begins. After some time, a sensual object tempts the Sadhaka. The inward struggle cease. The Sattvic mind is made inoperative. The higher mind forgets its duty; the lower mind ignores the danger. When this wave of excitement is over, then, once again, the struggle starts; but the vigour of the struggle is lost. The evil mind gets strengthened by the slackness of the Sattvic mind; and it becomes more and more difficult to subdue it.

Sadhaka! Be ever vigilant. Catch the thief of the lower mind and exterminate it.

PARABLE OF THE POOR MAN AND HIS TREASURE-TROVE

There was a poor man in a village who had an all-consuming desire to become rich. God took the form of a fortune-teller and told the poor man: "O man, dig a pit near the wall at the back of your house. You will find a rich treasure-trove in it." The poor man rejoiced greatly when this proved correct. Having obtained much wealth, the poor man relaxed and became indifferent to the acquisition or even maintenance of the wealth. Coming to know of his carelessness, one day a thief entered the house and carried away the treasure-trove. When the poor man found that his wealth was gone, he was terribly shocked. He cried himself hoarse and began running here and there in search of the treasure-trove. In the meantime, the same fortune-teller found the thief running away with the treasure-trove and caught hold of him; the treasure-trove was duly returned to the poor man, who rejoiced greatly. From that moment he never relaxed his vigilance and was ever guarding the treasure-trove and exerted himself to add to it.

Similarly, a good man aspires to realise God. His aspiration is so intense that God, in His Supreme Mercy and Compassion, sends him a Guru. The Guru points out that within the chambers of his heart resides the Supreme Bliss, God. The good man exerts himself and attains some measure of success in his Sadhana. This success turns his head and makes him relax his efforts. Finding him thus callous, Maya overpowers him and carries away his spiritual progress. He is where he was before he started Sadhana. He suddenly discovers this truth and laments over his fate. The Guru comes to him again and recaptures for him the experiences he had previously gained by Sadhana. He also warns him against being lax in Sadhana. From that moment, the good man never relaxes his vigilance. He guards the treasure-trove of spiritual experience that has been granted to him and exerts to add to it day after day. Once having known the consequences of non-vigilance, viz., great misery, he never relaxes his vigilance once again.

PARABLE OF THE WEEDS IN THE FIELD

A man sowed paddy in his fields. To his surprise he discovered after a week that though the paddy-crop had come up, there was a more abundant growth of weeds in the field. He wondered: "I have not sown any seeds for these weeds!" The seeds were there latent in the earth. When the farmer watered the paddy-seeds, the weeds grew in greater abundance. He pulled the weeds out. Again they grew. He went on pulling them out by the root; at the same time he protected the paddy-crop. And, the paddy-crop grew and the weeds when they had all been pulled out by the root, ceased to grow on the land. The harvest was rich and plentiful. The farmer rejoiced exceedingly.

Similarly, a Sadhaka engages himself in Japa and meditation; but he finds to his surprise that evil Vrittis manifest themselves in his mind. He wonders "I have not meditated upon these evil thought-forms. How do they arise within me?" They were there within the mind in a latent form. And they began to grow in the natural course of events. He pulls out the manifested evil Vrittis and thinks he is free from all evils. The Sadhana proceeds satisfactorily for some time, when the evil Vrittis manifest themselves vigorously once again. He is still more astonished. He cautions himself, as a little carelessness might destroy the entire crop of good Samskaras. Ceaseless vigilance is exercised by the Sadhaka and all evil Vrittis are pulled out. In due time the good Samskaras grow strong and unassailable; and the weeds—evil thoughts—pulled out in their entirety, vanish altogether. The Sadhaka attains Siddhi and rejoices in Samadhi.

PARABLE OF THE CHEATING POSTMASTER

A villager wrote to his son living in a town: "Please send me Rupees 10 every month for my expenses." The village postmaster saw his opportunity in this and added one 0 to the figure and made it 100. The villager's son went on sending Rs. 100 every month to his father; and the postmaster coolly pocketed Rs. 90 and gave only Rs. 10 to the father.

CONQUEST OF MIND 109

The postmaster's greed grew wilder! He induced the villager to write to his son for more money. The villager wrote, "Please send me Rs. 20 hereafter." The postmaster added a 0 and made it Rs. 200. His income was doubled thereby.

One day a Postal Inspector paid a surprise visit to the Post Office and found out that the Postmaster was enjoying himself thoroughly. He made enquiries from the local people and suspected mischief.

He asked the old villager: "What are your needs?"

He answered: "Rs. 20 a month."

"Why are you sending your father Rs. 200 a month, whereas he needs only Rs. 20?" the Inspector asked the son.

The enquiry revealed the Postmaster's trick. Promptly he was dismissed and punished severely. The old villager was saved from being robbed of his income.

It is the Prana in the body that needs food to sustain the body. The needs of the Prana are very few. But the tongue coming between the food and the Prana demands very much more! It demands delicious dishes—sweets, *chutnies, sambar, rasam* and *dosai*. The more it is catered to, the greater becomes its craving.

The Guru comes into the life of the man and points out to him that there is some fraud, and that all that he is eating is not really necessary for the sustenance of the Prana. The thief is caught and punished severely by fasting, saltless diet, etc. He is completely overcome. The Sadhaka becomes a Jitendriya.

PARABLE OF THE MAN WHO CUT THE COW'S UDDER

A foolish man had a good cow which yielded plenty of milk. He was astonished that day after day he could get from the cow eight seers of milk in the morning and an equal quantity in the evening. He noticed that all this milk had come from the same udder. He foolishly thought that the cow had a great storage of milk in the udder and that it was refusing to yield more than eight seers at a time. He was greedy and eager to have the whole milk at a time. One morning, therefore, he took a sharp razor and cut the cow's udder. He thought that by this method he could get the whole milk. What a tragedy! He got only profuse blood instead. Not a drop of milk was there in the udder. The cow bled to death.

Like this a foolish Sadhaka finds that Tapasya yields wonderful will-power and spiritual progress. But this progress is always gradual but steady and continuous. He is not satisfied with it. He wants the Highest Spiritual Experience to drop into his lap in a day. Then he begins to perform Asuri Tapasya. He takes the sharp razor of extreme austerity and cuts at the very life of Tapasya itself; and what does he get? Not spiritual progress, but downfall and death.

O man, practise Sattvic Tapasya. Follow the golden mean. Evolve step by step and enjoy Supreme Bliss.

PARABLE OF THE ADVOCATE'S TURBAN

An advocate was leaving the house in order to go to the Court. Just as he stepped on the road, he found that his turban was loose and as he took the next step, it collapsed. The entire length of the turban-cloth lay on the ground. He started tying it up again on his head. He could not. Every time he tried, he failed. He looked around. He discovered that at the foot of the staircase to his house there was a dome-light whose dome was of the size of his own head. He ran towards it and tied the turban around it, suggesting to himself that it was a head. Now he was perfectly successful. He then removed the neatly tied turban from the dome and placed it on his own head and walked away to the Court.

The man trying to leave this worldly atmosphere of pain and death, to go to the Court of the Supreme Monarch, God, finds that his turban (the mind) is loose. It is out of shape. It is all over the place. He tries to gather it together and make out of it a beautiful turban for his head; in other words, to do Samadhi with one-pointed mind and crown himself or to reach the Sahasrara at the crown of the head. Every time he tries, he fails. The Consciousness residing in the Sahasrara is too subtle for him to see and tie his mind upon. He looks around himself. He finds an image of the Lord. For a moment he feels that it is as good as God or the Supreme Consciousness itself. He fastens the mind on to this image. When all the mind has been firmly gathered on the image, then he quickly removes it from the image and raises it to the Sahasrara, to the Supreme Consciousness. Now he finds it easy. Then he walks away happily to the Court of the Supreme Monarch, God.

PARABLE OF A HUNDRED CHILDREN

There lived in a certain town two boy-friends, Rama and Krishna. They both were neighbours. Rama married a nice charming girl when he came of age, but Krishna remained a bachelor for a long time. Both Rama and Krishna inherited a lot of wealth from their parents. Rama multiplied his wealth and became a millionaire. But, Krishna adopted his spiritual friend and guide's son and lived within his own means very happily.

In spite of his increasing fortune, there was no happiness in Rama's house. Too many children born to him, were a regular source of constant annoyance to him and his wife. None of them could concentrate their attention on any of the children. The children always grew turbulent and boisterous and soon drained Rama of his wealth. No amount of income could help Rama to make both ends meet.

One day he approached Krishna and asked him as to the secret behind his happiness and the heavenly nature of his house. And Krishna replied, "I have but one son."

Rama and Krishna represent the human mind. One mind takes to some fancy, and begets a thousand desires as its offspring. The desires quickly drain the energy that the mind daily conserves through little concentration and meditation. The mind becomes a weakling, because of a number of desires. For the same reason, it cannot concentrate itself on a particular desire and achieve its end.

Krishna adopting the Guru's son is comparable to a mind imbibing a certain thought from the Guru and concentrating its energy and strength on developing it.

Where there are a thousand desires, there cannot be peace of mind or concentration of mental energy, or preservation even if it were only a weakling of mental strength. Where there is but a single desire, the mind can concentrate upon it well.

The greater the number of desires, the lesser is the peace and happiness. The lesser the desires, the greater is the peace of mind.

Learn to reduce the number of your desires. Keep one and one alone, and let that be divine. Concentrate the mind on it. You will enjoy peace and bliss; you will soon attain your goal.

CHAPTER EIGHT

THE PATH OF THE WISE

PARABLE OF THE GRAIN AND THE HAY

An agriculturist's young son accompanied his father to the field to watch the harvest. The father cut the laden corn, gathered it and brought it over to the backyard of the house. There he threshed the corn nicely, till the grains were separated from the stalk. Carefully he collected the grains and took them into the house where he stored them safely.

"Father, what about the hay that you have left in the backyard? You carried it from the field, but not into the house!" asked the boy.

"Son, the purpose of the hay is over. It had to carry the grain till the grain is separated from the stalk and taken possession of by us. When the grain has been collected, the hay has no more use for us. Then we only keep it to feed out cattle with." The son was well pleased with the lesson.

Even so, the Sastras yield the knowledge of the Self to the Sadhaka. Once Jnana is attained, the Sastras are of no more use to the Siddha. He carefully stores the Jnana within his heart and utilises his Sastric knowledge for the benefit of others who are yet leading a worldly life.

PARABLE OF FOUR LEARNED SCHOLARS

Once four learned scholars—an Ayurvedic doctor, an astrologer, a musician and a logician—had to spend a day at a village; and each was highly learned in his own science, a very great authority in his own subject, but empty of wisdom concerning life.

Now they went about collecting articles for their food, and the Ayurvedic doctor went to buy some vegetables. But he soon walked back home with empty hands, for his medical knowledge concerning the food-value of vegetables would not allow him to choose any. The potato was harmful as it would cause wind, while onion was too Tamasic and so did all other vegetables prove defective. And none was suitable for food.

The astrologer climbed a coconut tree to fetch a coconut for cooking. While he was climbing down, a donkey from a nearby house brayed, and lo, the astrologer stood on half-way down the tree, deciding at once to work out the astrological consequences of this donkey's braying! And he thus stood on...

The musician's history was yet more pathetic and ridiculous. He was watching the pot in which the rice was being cooked; the water was boiling, and soon a rythmic sound emanated from the boiling-pot. The musician, true and loyal to his knowledge of music, at once began marking time; but would the sound of the boiling-pot conform to the known laws of music? Soon the musician was beside himself in a fit of anger and broke the pot with the ladle, and lo the rice fell over the ground and was lost.

The logician was none the better for his erudition. He was returning with a cup full of ghee and *en route*, it struck his logic-loving mind to test and verify whether the cup supported the ghee or the ghee did the cup. He at once turned the cup upside down, and lo, the ghee fell on the ground, and was soon lost. Grief-stricken at the loss, yet the logician congratulated himself at the findings concerning the cup and the ghee and walked back home lost in thoughts of logic.

Be ye not merely learned, but become ye truly wise. For more learning will not bestow on you an iota of real happiness. Wisdom is bliss. Book-learning is lifeless knowledge; experience and true wisdom should be acquired through service of a Guru, studying under him and following his instructions in their true spirit.

PARABLE OF THE BOY AND THE CANDLE

The father and his little son are sitting in a dark room.

The son asks: "Father, I am afraid of this darkness. How can we remove it?"

"Light the candle, son."

The boy lights the candle. "Ah, now the darkness is gone, is it not Father?"

"Yes, son," replies the father. The son blows out the candle.

"Oh, it is again dark, father. I am afraid."

"Light the candle, son."

The boy lights the candle again. "Ah, now the darkness is gone."

This way he lights and blows off the candle several times.

Then the father tells him: "Son, so long as there is darkness, you should keep the candle burning. If you blow it off, the darkness will envelop you once again. But when the sun rises, you need the candle no more. Then you get light throughout the day from this supreme light of the universe."

Similarly, the disciple approaches the Guru for instruction on Yoga and receives the Diksha. The disciple practises Sadhana for a little while and gets a little spiritual progress. Satisfied that he has attained the Supreme and conquered Maya, he stops the Sadhana. Darkness envelops him again! This goes on—"Yoga comes and goes"—till he learns to be steadfast in his Sadhana. Thus he keeps the darkness of Maya away till the Sun of Atma-Jnana arises in him. With the rise of the Sun of Supreme Wisdom, the darkness of ignorance vanishes for ever, and he basks in the sunshine of Sahaja Samadhi.

PARABLE OF THE PEOPLE WHO DIED OF FEAR

A traveller in the middle-east met a curious fellow in the course of his journey. "Who are you?" he said, "and where are you going?" "I am Cholera. I am going to kill five thousand people in Egypt," said the other and resumed his journey. A few years later they again happened to meet together. The former asked the latter, "You had given me word to kill only five thousand people; but you have killed fifty thousand, instead." "No, No," he retorted, "I have killed only five thousand people; the rest died of fear."

The parable shows how fear is the deadly enemy of man. Ninety per cent of our worries and miseries are due to fear and wrong imagination. Though what is feared may never happen, yet the apprehension of it saps out the vitality of man. Only a *Brahmavit* is totally free from fear.

Fear is the product of ignorance. The Atman in its real nature is always fearless, diseaseless and free. One should realise the Atman and cross the ocean of fear, disease and miseries.

CHAPTER NINE

THE NATURE OF THE JIVANMUKTA

PARABLE OF THE HUNTER'S DREAM

A hunter went to bed at night and dreamt. In the dream he saw that a fierce lion was chasing him and was about to jump at him. He was frightened. He gave out a terrible cry. He dreamt that he was stooping to pick up his bow and arrow, shouting at his comrade "Get me bow and arrow." Actually, he slipped out of his bed in an effort to get the bow and arrow. At once he woke up. His son who was sleeping in the adjacent room, had heard his cry and his words: "Get me the bow and arrow." He did not know what it was all about and so rushed in with bow and arrow. The father smiled and shook his head: "No; I do not want them now. It was a dream only. Now that I know it was a dream, I have no more use for the bow and arrow. What a wonderful dream it was; though now I am awake and realise it was all a dream, I do still remember the dream vividly and rejoice."

Similarly, the Jiva lies down on the bed of the body. He dreams or imagines that he is roaming in the forest of this world. Great misery in the shape of disease, poverty, old age, etc., attacks him. He cries and shouts. He is wont on such occasions to take the weapon of sensual indulgence in a vain attempt to kill the misery. But the Grace of God takes him away from the body-consciousness. He attains Jnana. His friends and relatives treat him as they used to treat him before. But he smiles and declines to indulge the senses. He is an awakened soul. He now knows that his past life was but a long dream. In his awakened soul there is no misery at all; and therefore sense-indulgence has no meaning for him. Though he recalls the memory of his past life of ignorance, he now realises that it was all a long dream, fit only to be laughed over.

PARABLE OF THE TORCH IN A DARK ROOM

A man entered his room when it was dark. He wanted to take his torchlight which he knew was in the room. He began to search for it. He tumbled over many things; he knocked his head here and there. Lo! The torchlight is in his grasp now. Instantly the darkness vanishes and he is able to move about in the room with freedom and ease.

A Sadhaka enters the dark caverns of his inner self, where he knows the Light of the Self lies. During his search he seems to stumble and fall, and knock his head here and there. At last the moment arrives—the great Moment of moments—and the light is within his grasp. Instantly ignorance vanishes. The Light of the Self is upon his soul. No more struggle; no more trouble. He moves about freely as a Jivanmukta.

PARABLE OF THE CHILD AND THE SHADOW

The elder brother thought that his baby brother was alone in the room adjoining the kitchen. Suddenly

THE NATURE OF THE JIVANMUKTA

he heard the child laughing, playing and talking. Before his mental eye rose the image of a thief entering the house, offering a few sweetmeats to the baby and of his snatching away the golden ornaments with which they had adorned the baby. With great consternation, the brother rushed into the room in which the baby was. What did he find there? The baby was playing with its own shadow cast on the wall. The brother was pacified, hugged the child with great love.

Similarly, the worldly man busy in his world, looking after the affairs of the stomach, feels that the Sadhu is a lonely being in another part of the Lord's mansion. Suddenly he discovers that there is much laughter and 'life' in the Sadhu's camp. The worldly man sunk in ignorance imagines that the thief of Maya has entered the camp of the Sadhu, and that, offering him a few comforts and conveniences, it has robbed the Sadhu of the valuable ornaments of Vairagya, Viveka and spiritual illumination. With these thoughts haunting him, the worldly man takes a closer look at the Sadhu. The Jivanmukta is playing with his own shadows. In the eyes of the Jivanmukta all Jivas in the world are but his own shadows. In playing with them he takes an intense delight. He has neither gained anything, nor lost anything. Only the worldly man imagines so.

PARABLE OF THE FIRE'S POLLUTION

A man had taken food. He was suffering from a terrible disease. He took the leaf in which he had taken his food and, wishing to avoid polluting the society with it, threw the leaf in a fire burning nearby. An orthodox

Brahmin witnessing this scene grew indignant and felt that the fire had thus been polluted. He did not know what to do, but felt that something should be done. What does man do when he is polluted? He pours water on his head (bathes). Unthinkingly this orthodox Brahmin poured water on the fire, to purify it! The fire was promptly put out; and the rubbish that it was meant to burn away remained. Another intelligent Brahmin pointed out the orthodox man's foolishness, and said: "What a great harm have you done! How can fire, the purifier of all, be polluted? That man who threw the leaf into the fire was quite right. If he had not done so, the entire society would be infected with his fell disease. Fire would burn up all the disease germs. But, by imagining that the fire was polluted and by thus putting the fire out, you have only brought trouble on us all! The great work of purification that the fire was doing has been suspended." Then he brought back the fire again, lit the rubbish-heap and reduced it to ashes.

The fire is comparable to a Jivanmukta. He burns up all that is sinful and evil in all beings. His light burns bright among sinners and wicked men. He burns away their sins and transforms them into the pure ash of Jnana. A notorious wicked man comes to the Jivanmukta and in order to earn his grace offers his wealth or house to the Jivanmukta. When the orthodox worldly man looks at this, he is puzzled. He thinks that the Jivanmukta has been tainted by this villain's sins. He actually feels that the Jivanmukta himself has become a wicked man! Thinking thus, he ill-treats the Jivanmukta and makes him leave the place. What happens, then? The evil-minded men who were being reformed by the Jivanmukta's divine presence once again reign supreme in the locality. Adharma fills the atmosphere. A wise man comes into the scene and chastises the orthodox, foolish man. He says: "How foolish of you to believe that the Jivanmukta could be polluted by the wickedness of the villain! What do you know of the all-purifying nature of the Jivanmukta? Nothing can taint him. He does not refuse to bless anyone. He gladly and joyously consumes the sins of all. The wicked man was right in going to the lotus-feet of the Jivanmukta and offering his wealth and building to the Jivanmukta. The latter would purify everything. But, by driving him away, you have only brought untold evil upon the entire society." Then this wise man brings back the Jivanmukta who once again begins to carry on his mission of purifying the souls of wicked men.

PARABLE OF THE COWS AND THE SCRATCHING PILLAR

Every day in a village the cows used to be taken out for grazing. After grazing for a couple of hours, the cows would gather around the cowherd for their necks to be scratched. The intelligent cowherd had set up a contrivance for this purpose. It was a pillar with a little rough surface. The cows would go to this pillar and scratch their necks to their satisfaction and joy.

Similarly, a Jivanmukta leads many Jivas into the rich pastures of Sadhana for God-realisation. They are not able remain immersed in meditation all the twenty-four hours. The Rajasic temperament manifests to itself and they become restless. They crave for satisfaction of this 'nerve-itching' also. Therefore, the Jivanmukta creates an institution. The Jivas get busy with this institution. They get great relief. The Jivanmukta looks on with delight and satisfaction; he remains a blissful Sakshi of this play. He is not attached to the institution which has been created only for the sake of the aspiring souls.

PART TWO
OTHER PARABLES

PART TWO
OTHER PARABLES

PARABLE OF RAJA JANAKA AND THE PANDITS

Some Pandits criticised Raja Janaka:
"Raja Janaka is a worldly man.
How can he be a Jnani or a Sage?"
Raja Janaka wanted to teach them a lesson,
He called all Pandits
And gave them a very good feast.
Many tasty preparations were served,
All the Pandits were rejoicing.
But to their astonishment,
They saw a sword hanging above their heads,
The sword was tied by means of a hair.
They all trembled.
They all mixed everything and ate hurriedly.
When the feast was over
They came to the Durbar.
Raja Janaka asked:
"O Pandits, what things did you eat today?
Were they all nice, according to your taste?"
The Pandits replied;
"Our minds were on the hair only.
We do not know anything."
Janaka said:
"O Pandits, similar is the state of my mind.
My mind is fixed on Brahman alone;
I do not know anything of this world."
The Pandits put down their heads in shame.
They now realised the state of a Jivanmukta.
The Jivanmukta may appear
To be doing the normal duties of life.

But his mind is not in the world;
It is unified with the Absolute.

PARABLE OF THE OLD LADY AND THE NEEDLE

One old lady lost a needle in the house,
But she was searching for it outside
In the moonlight.
One man asked her:
"O lady, what are you searching here?"
She replied: I lost a needle in the house;
There is darkness inside;
So I am searching for the needle here."
Worldly people are like this old lady.
They are searching for happiness in the object,
Where real happiness does not exist.
Look within; control the mind;
You will find the object of your quest
                              in your own Atman.

PARABLE OF THE MOTHER-IN-LAW AND THE BEGGAR

A beggar came to the house when the mother-in-law was away and the daughter-in-law refused to give alms. The beggar went away. The mother-in-law met him on the road. He told her that her daughter-in-law had refused to give his alms. "What right had she?" roared the mother-in-law, "come with me." The beggar came back to the house, full of expectation. As soon as she reached the house, she turned round and said: "Get away. I won't give you alms. But even for this refusal only I have the right in this house and not my daughter-in-law."

Even so, when a man turns away from the objects of the world, out of disgust, the spiritual preceptor admonishes him and point out to him that he should not remain inactive, or shun the world. For a while, he seems to preach activism, on the theory that the world is a solid reality! He asked the Sadhaka to work, to serve all and to love all, as though the 'many' exist. In due course, the Sadhaka attains Self-realisation. Then he abandons all worldliness, truly renounces the world, and remains immersed in the Consciousness of the One. But here the renunciation is born of Self-realisation. He has the authority to renounce; and he alone can renounce the world and all activity. He has realised the One Self in all. The aspirant has Ajnana-Vairagya, Vairagya generated by the painful nature of the world; the saint has Jnana-Vairagya or Vairagya born of the realisation of the essential nature of the Self which is One, Indivisible, All-pervading Consciousness, the Great Indwelling Presence, realising which man longs for nothing else.

PARABLE OF THE YOUNG MAN'S BOON

There was once a young man who lived in a village nearby a temple. He used to love God only for Prasad and for ringing the bells. His love for the Divine was innocent and unknowing. He used to think of the carved and installed stone as God. He used to revere as such and pray: "O God! Grant me whatever I want and whenever I want. I shall feel ever happy and eternally beholden to Thee for ever." He knew no other prayer except this.

One day the Lord much pleased with his guileless and open-hearted devotion appeared in his dream and asked: "Do you want to enjoy your will and wishes up to the time of pensionable age when afterwards there will be none to help you or a care free, happy mendicant's life with just a day's morsel every day and enough clothing and shelter?"

Due to the natural delusion of youth, he said: "My Lord! I prefer the former." The Lord granted it. The joy of the man knew no bounds. He thought he would be happy by getting all he needed at the required moments. Poor fellow! Once he prayed "O Lord! Grant me good education without any impediments." It was readily granted.

Again, "O Bhagavan! Help to have daily a seer each of Mysore Pak, Bengal Rasagullas, Sandilla Laddus, Rishikesh Kheer and Masula Zilebi." The Lord said "Be it so. You will have them now at this very second" for the third time. "O Almighty! Permit me to enjoy wife and children. I am in dire need of marriage. Look to my bodily comforts." The Lord sanctioned that, too.

Again after some time, "O Sweet Providence! I want to go to Badrinath. Kindly look to my case and provide me with all the necessaries." The Lord said: "All right. Take utensils, clothes, money and other requirements."

The devotee became puffed up with pride in due course and began to command the Lord even. "O Thou

OTHER PARABLES

Devadev! Make me master over Thee." The Lord, guessing his wish beforehand, disappeared to avoid turning down his response.

Years rolled on thus. The more the desires were fulfilled, the more he used to ask. The Lord wanted to turn his mind towards His side and so He made him ask, making him forget the stipulation of his original boon, for the last time when the age of superannuation already approached: "My Lord! My years are waning. My wife has become old and haggard, nonchalant and non-responsive. My children have gone abroad. But yet my mind is bent on enjoying life as there are only a few years left. I want to relish life still to my heart's content before I leave this body." Then the Lord said: "Be your wish fulfilled." He was then leading a reckless, dissipated life lest he should let waste what is left to him. He knew not day or night in sensual pleasures. His life of love lay in enjoyment. But he was attacked by an incurable disease. Weeping and crying and bawling aloud became regular day-to-day features with him. There is none to approach him or help him. He is now in dotage. The age of superannuation greeted him. The cursed days approached.

He wept and wailed and at last resolved to make an end to his life by jumping down the bridge far from his village, with the flowing river underneath. In the dead of night he went there groping in darkness. He cursed himself once again for not having chosen the latter course while asking for the boon in dream. Pouring forth his heart once more unto Him he was ready to jump down recklessly in a fraction of a second when he felt a strong irresistible backward pull from behind. There was none to be seen to the right or left or at the back. On turning round in a fit of frenzy and disgust, in a welling cataclysm of sorrow and disappointment he saw a blazing fire at a distance. Now there was a magnetic pull towards the fire to lose his life therein. He knew not why it was so. He felt inwardly that somebody was calling out to him. He now directed his steps towards the fire. On the way he trod over a wriggling, crawling snake. He lit a match. Lo! It was not a snake but a rope, he cursed himself and God for having lost another chance to embrace death. He proceeded onwards towards the fire. As he was fast approaching unmindful of his own self, there was light greater and greater in intensity of brightness as he paced each step forward. The more he walked, the more distant it seemed. It was nearing dawn. Again he resolved to drop himself down into a distantly seeming well but lo! when he approached the spot the fire disappeared and an anchorite, from inside the cottage with a shining lustrous face appeared and said: "Life is not for deliberate death. How ignorant thou art to try to make an end of thyself! Give up such idea. Did I not ask you on that night to choose fruition of desires as and when they arise till none would help thee in old age or a happy desire-proof ascetic life? Make amends even now. No man of desires is ever happy. They multiply as minutes pass by. The secret of fulfilment of desires lies in utter renunciation thereof. I pity thee. Go thou to the yonder rivulet and have thy bath. It is now Brahmamuhurta. Come quick. I shall initiate thee into Knowledge of Brahman by which thou becomest desire-cum-disease-free and become one with me. Sit beside me and pray. You shine as Bliss Absolute."

So saying, the Sadhu sent him away to the rivulet and then disappeared. On return from the watery source, the old man found out none, neither the cottage nor the anchorite except a Hamsa Danda, a Kamandalu, a Kaupeen and a deerskin all in one beside a pit of fire with none around. He searched and searched for the Sadhu but all in vain. He returned back to the Dhun quite dejected. He was now in a perplexing mood and was at his wit's end as to what to do next. Then a Voice from above said: "Sweet Beloved Self! I help those in distress wherever they be by my Resplendent Effulgence. The fire thou saw from the Bridge is I myself. I am thee. But thou art not I. I am in thee, I am with thee and I am around thee. Fear not. Remember me ever. I shall guide thee unto Me. There is nothing for thee to shrink. I know what is passing in thy mind. I want to make thee one with Me, the Fire of Effulgence thou saw.

He now realised Lord's Will by the emblems present there and took Sannyasa to repeat OM and become one with OM.

PARABLE OF THE SADHU AND THE SWORD

A king was crossing a jungle. On the way he felt extremely thirsty. He wanted to take a refreshing bath also. He entered the hermitage of an old Tapasvin and asked him: "Maharaj, is there any river or lake nearby in which I can take bath and refresh myself?"

"Yes, there is a river, a hundred yards to the east of this hermitage. Its waters are cool and refreshing. Please do take your bath in it. It is purifying and holy, too."

"In that case, Maharaj, can I leave my luggage here? What is the use of carrying all this about?"

"All right, you may keep it here. Oh, what is that glittering thing?" he asked looking at the golden scabbard which the king handed him.

The king unsheathed the gleaming sword which the hermit admired in his child-like simplicity. The king understood that hermit had not seen a sword before, in his life-time, and merely warning him, "Please be careful not to meddle with this," went away.

The Tapasvin was soon tempted to find out the properties of the sword. He unsheathed it and placed it on the ground. It at once cut the soft Kusa-grass bed on which he was sitting. The Tapasvin grew more curious. He took sword in his hand and struck a water-melon lying in front of him; the water-melon was cut into two. Two deer were playing in front of the Kutir; the Tapasvin threw the sword at them. It hit one of them and that one was instantly killed. At this moment the king returned from his bath. He was indignant that Tapasvin should thus have misused the weapon. His Kshatriya assertive nature prompted him to use a few hot words; and the Tapasvin at once rushed towards the king, sword in hand. But the wise king shot an arrow at the Tapasvin and severed the hand holding the sword. The Tapasvin at once realised the terrible mistake he had committed.

The Yogi practises deep meditation. He advances in Raja Yoga. After some practice, this Raja Yoga gives him some wonderful Siddhis. The Yogi tries to use the Siddhis for some simple and harmless purpose. He finds that he can get rid of simple ailments with his Yogic powers. He is able to keep ferocious animals under his control so that they won't harm him. He is also able to influence some human beings and make them serve him. From one experiment to the other, he proceeds with the use of his psychic powers. When he discovers that his psychic powers are enormous, then he stops his Sadhana, he gives up his Tapasya and goes headlong down the abyss of delusion. He is ready to cut even the throat of the Yoga itself; he is ready to destroy the very Sadhana that gave him the psychic powers. But, in time God's Grace descends into him and cuts off the evil promptings within him which make use of his psychic powers. The Yogi realises his serious mistake and thenceforward never runs after the Siddhi. He attains to the Supreme Peace.

PARABLE OF THE BOY WHO COULD NOT TELL THE TIME

A man asked a boy: "Little one, tell me what the time is now."

"Uncle, I cannot read the clock."

"I see; for how long have you been ignorant of this?"

The boy was silent; he could not answer this question. "God knows, uncle." He replied and kept mum.

Some intellectually proud people question the simple saints: "Since when has Avidya been veiling the Truth? Or, when did Avidya originate?" These questions are unanswerable; they are transcendental questions. The little mind cannot answer them. Silence is the answer. "God only knows."

PARABLE OF THE BIRD AND THE COTTON-FRUIT

A bird has its nest on the branch of a cotton-tree. Near the nest there was an unripe fruit. Every day it would look at it and think: "Let it ripen; then I will eat it." It waited and waited. Suddenly one day, even as it was eagerly looking, the fruit burst and its content flew away! The bird was sorely disappointed.

A young man thinks that when he grew old he would practise Sadhana. Days roll by. Suddenly one fine morning life departs from the body. He had spent his life in vain.

Therefore, take time by the forelock; do it now.

PARABLE OF THE MAN IN
THE PYTHON'S MOUTH

Two men were walking along the jungle-path. One man was going a furlong ahead of the other. The man walking ahead was suddenly caught hold of by a huge python which was swallowing him. The other man hesitated and stood where he was. The first man, with half his body swallowed by the python began shouting at the other: "You fool, why are you standing there hesitant? Come I am here to lead you and protect you."

Similarly, man has been caught by the huge python of Maya. He is being swallowed by this terrible creature. Yet, such is the height of his delusion, he boasts that he can protect others and that he can guide and lead them along to safety and happiness!

PARABLE OF THE BOY AND THE ANGEL

There was a very hard-working student who used to study till late in the night. He was very poor. He had to exert much for getting books and oil for his midnight studies. One day, being much tired, he fell asleep at night, while he was at his studies. He saw in his dream a strange vision. A celestial being appeared to him and said: "O boy, open your mouth and I shall put into it a pill of all the knowledge of the universe. Thus be relieved of all your troubles, and rest in peace." But the boy said: "I want not all the knowledge of the universe to be spat into my mouth. Be gracious enough to provide me with oil for my studies." Thus, the vision ended and the boy, by his self-exertion, became one of the greatest men of the age.

A Sadhaka, too, must have the same spirit of self-exertion. Then alone will he evolve quickly and attain to the peak of knowledge. A mother can give food to the son, but she cannot herself digest it for him. He has to digest it himself. A Guru or guide can show one the right path, but one has to tread it oneself.

Expect not to acquire knowledge without any exertion on your part, for verily such knowledge is mere dream. Right exertion alone can enable you to draw grace from Guru or God. One who flies away from difficulties can never be relieved of them. But one who faces them boldly will afterwards be able to cross them and will attain supreme Peace and Bliss even in this very life.

PARABLE OF WATER AND FIRE

Once Fire met Water on the banks of the Ganga to settle an age-long dispute between them as to which of them was powerful. Water asserted its prowess by quoting ample incidents in support of its ability to put down even big fires and told that Fire could not do anything to water save only when water is confined to small vessels.

That much of a hint was enough for Fire. Knowing fully well that it could not score a direct victory over Water, Fire digressed a bit and began to talk about the welfare of Water. It said, "My dear Water, look! how much dirt is there around you. Why not you just step into this beautiful golden vessel. It will help you to remain ever pure and clean." Water was naturally tempted; and no sooner did he jump into the golden vessel, than Fire boiled it with all its might. As it was becoming warmer and warmer, Water found everything comfortable. When once the boiling point was reached, water felt the torture and began to brood over its folly.

Sivananda Says:

It is all a parable.

Like the Water your pure thoughts, your discriminative intellect, your reason, nay, your Mumukshutva and love for soul is.

Nothing can defile it as long as it goes its own way. It is ever pure and clean. It has got the power to cleanse everything.

Like the Fire, your love for flesh is.

Fire is ferocious. So too, love for flesh.

It is equally powerful like Water. If one annihilates the other all at once, the other has got the ability to torture the first.

O Man, safeguard your Mumukshutva, your reason, your discriminative intellect. It is ever powerful.

The love for flesh tempts you to seek little comforts. You feel you are comfortable and unattached to the comforts at the same time. The comforts increase slowly and slowly like the water getting warmer and warmer. You feel all right. But, when it comes to the boiling point, you feel. You brood over your follies. You become a complete slave to the luxurious things. You lose your power and ability to put down the fire of lust, greed, etc.

In short, you are lost.

The love for flesh is ever on the alert to seek its little comforts. It pleads and tempts at every moment your

Sattvic mind and intellect. Never, never hear it. Be careful. Assert the supreme power of your aspiration, your love for soul. You will be intact and unaffected by the fire that is the lower nature in you, that is the old evil Vasanas.

PARABLE OF THE OPIUM-SMOKERS AND MOON'S REFLECTION

On a moonlit night three opium smokers were wandering in search of fire to light up their cigars. In course of their wanderings they happened to pass by the side of a river. The reflection of the moon was playing with the ripples of the river. It shone like fire. They sent one of them to ignite a charcoal piece from the fire. He went near the river and placed the charcoal on the ripples, but he found it cool. He had to return without success. The others rebuked him saying that he ought to have gone a bit further, for the fire was a bit further than that. Another started to ignite it. He entered into the river a bit further but also had to return without success. The third thinking himself to be the wisest entered into the river upto the middle of it, but the fire was not there. He also had to return without securing any success in his attempts.

The nature of Samsara is also like that of the illusory fire. In the night of ignorance the Jivas intoxicated by the opium of desires search for momentary pleasures. The desires constitute real Karmas which bind the individual souls to the earthly plane. The sensual pleasure here is but the reflection of Satchidananda. As long as the mystery is not realised the Jivas run after illusory things thinking them to be the real. One may collect more of the facts regarding the phenomenal universe and boast oneself for knowing more than the ancestors. But such boastings are in vain. One who enters upto the middle of the river for igniting the charcoal is as much a fool as one who remains only by the side of it.

He alone knows who knows not the reflection but the moon. He alone knows who knows the futility of sensual pleasures and the false nature of the universe. Only Satchidananda is all this. Differences exist only due to Avidya or ignorance. A Brahmavid crossing over Avidya becomes Brahman Himself.

PARABLE OF THE HUSBAND AND THE WIFE

There once happily lived a poor couple in a little village. Whenever the wife brooded over their poverty and pressed the husband to procure enough things to lead a decent life in uniformity with the rest of the villagers, the husband used to reply that the Lord loved them most and that is why He had kept them in that poor state. Through blandishment, coquetry and crocodile tears, as women are wont to do, the wife reduced the husband to a mere slave in the long run. One day she sent him to a generous friend of his, commanding him to offer a handful of water to his friend as a present. Without any alternative, the husband did the same. His generous friend, knowing fully well the devotee's poverty, amply rewarded the hands that offered a little water with love and devotion. But, the poor man lost his devotional aspect and began to think, "If a little water can fetch me a handful of wealth, what I would have received, had I only offered a potful of water."

Sivananda Says:

Look into this Parable.

Thy Buddhi is like the husband, and thy physical being is like the wife. They are destined to live together happily like Man and Woman.

It is the duty of the wife to procure the little domestic needs. Her world is confined only to that. It is the duty of the husband to guide her and lead her properly. But, when the wife displays her crocodile tears, the husband loses his brain and trying to comfort her, willingly obeys her forgetting his own duty and integrity.

Thy physical being, too, craves for its little comforts. Your Viveka tries to convince it that they are useless. But, when it pleads and weeps before you, you allow it a little freedom and choice. Instead of trying to check it, you pacify it. In doing so, you yourself fall a victim to its snares.

O Man, wake up. Do not allow your Viveka to become a slave to your love for flesh, for your body. Mercilessly turn down the demands of your body for little comforts. If once you allow it the use of little comforts and you also taste them, it is very difficult for you to assert the superiority of your Viveka over your lower nature.

You cannot divorce your body. Viveka and Vichara are possible only in the human body.

The wife is not merely a mistress to the husband for giving carnal pleasures. She is not a mere creature, but the glory of God's creation that should help you to know Him.

Utilise this body to know and realise God without becoming a slave to it. Otherwise, you are lost. Read the story of 'The Husband and Wife' once again.

PARABLE OF THE PET CHILD

Once a mother engaged a tutor for her mischievous but pet boy. She could not tolerate the tutor scolding the boy. So, she engaged another tutor for her boy. The new tutor began to beat the boy in order to correct him and make him good. The mother wished to have her son's manners corrected and cultured but could not suffer the sight of the son being put to trouble with arduous task and punishments. She was neither willing to send the son away to school; for, it meant being separated from the son for some time during the day. All her efforts were directed to keeping the boy attractive.

As days passed by and years rolled on, tutor after tutor came and went but the brain of the boy remained as it was when it came into this world; nevertheless, the boy grew into a handsome youth and thence into a man. He could not pull on in this world, for he had neither intelligence nor money, neither capacity to work nor good manners to pull on with the remaining members of either his family or of the society at large. People scoffed at him and condemned him. He was lost to himself and to the world.

Sivananda Says:

Like the mother, your aspiration is. Your body and external habits are like the mischievous son.

You wish to make yourself a great spiritual hero in the eyes of the public. You go from teacher to teacher, because you cannot undergo the ordeal of patiently obeying any teacher. You do not like to strain the body. You think that if you maintain an external show with a well developed body, with beard and matted locks you will pass for a good man. Your Abhimana to the body is so great that you cannot forget it for a few minutes and sit in Sadhana. In your wandering from Guru to Guru, you have not been able to assimilate anything. Remember, 'A rolling stone gathers no moss.'

You go about into the world without intelligence or capacity. You cannot tune yourself to any society. You have been lost to yourself and to the world at large.

O Man, practise Sadhana while you are young. Leave out this Abhimana for body. Undergo a little initial hardship. It is no hardship when compared to the bliss that you shall reap as the harvest.

PARABLE OF THE MAN AND HIS MUD-HORSE

A highly intellectual young man had his bicycle converted into a beautiful looking horse. The horse was made of mud. When he rode the bicycle, it appeared that he was riding the mud-horse. He went on pretending it was a horse with mysterious powers and could do as well as any horse could. He went on joy-rides along with his comrades who rode real horses. One day, they were about to cross a stream. The man with the mud-horse thought within himself: "When pots are immersed in water, they remain intact. Even so, my horse will remain intact even in water. I can cross this stream." He got into the stream. When he was in mid-stream, the mud-horse collapsed, drowning the rider and burying him in the river-bed. The others understood that the horse was made of unbaked mud and went their way.

With a little intelligence, a Sadhaka gets by heart some texts and their commentaries. He pretends that he has mysterious powers and more mysterious Jnana. He always rides abreast with Brahma-Jnanis and talks on equal terms with them. The path is beset with many dangers and trials. The pretender cannot stand even a single trial. At the crucial moment, his intelligence vanishes, his knowledge deserts him and his Vairagya gives way. His Vairagya has not been baked properly in the fire of Viveka and Mumukshutva. He perishes miserably, while the real Jnanis and Yogis fearlessly and joyously surmount all obstacles and overcome all dangers.

PARABLE OF THE PHILOSOPHER AND THE BROKEN MIRROR

Once there lived two friends, Ram and Gopal. They were both philosophers. By Vichara and Anvaya-vyatireka, Ram learned to see the Glory of the Supreme Self reflected in and through all the universe. But Gopal continued to remain a theoretical philosopher, condemning the universe as an illusion and dream containing nothing but evil and vice.

One day, after a long time, Ram called on his friend. Gopal discussed for a long time, as usual, the evil in this universe, and in the end asked Ram what present he had brought for his friend. Ram, after thinking a while, produced a broken piece of mirror from his pocket and handing it over to Gopal, said, "This is my little and humble present. It will help you to understand your own beauty and charm, which you cannot otherwise see."

Gopal learnt a lesson, and from that moment began to visualise and understand the Glory of the Supreme Self reflected in all the universe.

Nothing is useless in this world.

The non-self exists to reflect and glorify the Self. Otherwise how can you know the existence of the Self?

Verily, the non-self is the mirror that truly reflects the Self for us to cognise.

So, too, evil is the mirror for good. The presence of sages and saints is easily cognised amidst an assembly of ignorant men.

Learn to see the good reflected by the evil, and say, "Evil exists to remind me of good, the perishable exists to remind me of the Imperishable," and so on.

Truly, this universe is a mirror that reminds us of God. Learn not to condemn it as an illusion and dream, but to utilise it to feel the presence of God.

PARABLE OF THE BRAHMIN
WHO ESCAPED RAIN

An old Brahmin was walking along the road when it began to rain heavily. He had no umbrella. He was afraid of catching cold. There was no place to take shelter, too. He saw at a distance two coolies carrying a wooden cot. He ran forward. He was shorter than the coolies. He went between the two coolies, with the wide cot over his head. Not a drop of rain fell on his head. Occasionally he also helped the coolies a little; but the advantage to him was very much more than the labour.

Many Sadhakas expose themselves to the severe rain of worldly temptations, while they are walking towards the destination—God-realisation. The wise ones, discover an intelligent way of escaping the evil effects of these temptations. They find that there exist very near them Ashrams and spiritual institutions managed by spiritually "taller" souls, more advanced Sadhakas and saints. By joining such Ashrams and institutions, they escape the temptations and trials. The advanced souls carry a protective shield underneath which the lesser souls take refuge and thus avoid getting lost. These aspirants also contribute a little to the institutions; but eventually the advantage they derive is something very great, in comparison to the work they contribute. Such is the glory of spiritual institutions.

PARABLE OF THE CONDUCTOR
WHO FELL OFF THE BUS

The bus had started. The conductor noticed, as he was standing on the foot-board, that a man was running towards the bus. In his "compassion", he held out his hand. The man came running and caught hold of the conductor. As he was heavier than the conductor, the moment he caught hold of the conductor's hand, the conductor himself was pulled away from the bus and he found himself on the road. Now both of them began to run towards the bus. A hefty passenger who was securely sitting inside the bus now held out his hands through the window; both of them caught hold of his hands and jumped on to the bus.

This happens very often in the aspirant's journey to the Goal. As he stands on the foot-board of Sadhana which he has just ascended, he thinks too much of his strength and goes about "saving" other people. The result is obvious. He himself is pulled on to the road of worldly life. The beginner has no business to try to help wicked people reform themselves; he should mind his own Sadhana. If he meddles in other people's affairs, he too becomes worldly-minded; then he, too, has to run towards the bus of Sadhana. An advanced Sadhaka or saint comes to his rescue. He is established in Sadhana. Even he does not take the risk of coming out of the fortress of Sadhana in order to help other aspirants. He still remains firm in his Sadhana and holds out his hand through the window of selfless service. Other aspirants are thus taken on the bus of spiritual Sadhana. This is the best method.

PARABLE OF THE MANAGER WHO REMOVED THE HANDS OF THE CLOCK

In an office the staff was ever eager to see that it struck 5 p.m. and one more day's salary earned without working for it. The manager noticed that every few minutes after 4 the members of the staff were again and again looking at the office-clock to see if the clock had struck 5. Quietly he went over to the clock and removed the two hands. Afterwards, the members of the staff worked with calm interest and counted, not the hours and minutes, but the work that they were able to turn out.

In the world, a selfish man is ever eager to see that whether he has rendered any good action or not, he got good reward. If he gives a cup of water, he looks eagerly forward to a reward or at least an expression of gratitude. Noticing this, the Guru comes into the man's life and removes the two hands of this clock of selfishness—attachment to action and longing for the fruits of actions. Afterwards the man works for work's sake, never expecting any reward but ever conscious of his duty.

PARABLE OF THE BOY AND HIS SHOES

The dog barked at him and the boy began to run. The dog began to chase him. The boy found that his shoes were impeding his speed. He let them slip off his feet. He left them behind. The dog instantly caught hold of one of the shoes and ran away from the boy who then proceeded home safely.

The world troubles the man in every way, so long as he possesses the two things—I-ness and mine-ness. With egoism and possessive nature, wherever he runs, the miseries of Samsara chase him and leave him no respite. Attached to a thousand things, he also is not able to proceed towards his destination with expedition. Therefore, he renounces the I-ness and mine-ness, in order to proceed faster towards the goal. As soon as he renounces the possessions, the world gives up chasing him and the miseries of Samsara leave him once for all. Renunciation has this double advantage: it relieves you of all burdens, lightens your heart and thus enables you to soar higher into the spiritual realm, and it also enables you to free yourself from the troubles of friends and relatives. Therefore, renounce the world and enjoy Supreme Bliss.

PARABLE OF THE MASKED BOY AND THE MOUSE

A boy put on the mask of a frightful giant and went to the place where other boys were playing. He uttered frightening cries; and the boys afraid of this demon, flew away. Suddenly the masked boy himself began to wail aloud. He fell down and crawled out of the mask. There was a mouse within the mask; and the boy was terribly afraid of it!

An aspirant puts on the mask of a Self-realised sage and delivers thundering discourses trying to reform all the people, people are struck with awe and wonder. Very soon, the aspirant has a downfall; and the mask of pseudo-Jnana is also broken. Because, there is the mouse of lust, anger, greed and hypocrisy within, which exposes his weakness and reveals his true, timid, foolish nature. O aspirant, beware of hypocrisy. Be sincere and attain the Goal.

PARABLE OF THE CHILDREN'S QUARREL OVER MUD-HOUSES

Several children were playing on the village street, building houses and acting the part of families etc. One child got annoyed with another and in a fit of anger kicked the house built by the latter. The two began to quarrel over this. "You have destroyed my house; how dare you?" etc., etc. A young man who was watching all this began to laugh at the children's foolishness in quarrelling over the imaginary "houses" made of a handful of mud which were in any case to be destroyed after the play came to an end. An elderly man, however, remarked: "Friend, when you were a young boy, you, too, quarrelled like that. Now that you have grown old, you no more take interest in these things. You have acquired the sense of proper valuation of things. Come. let us by all means pacify the children; but you should not laugh at their behaviour."

Similarly, in the world people quarrel over the petty things. They build houses of brick and mud; and quarrel over their possession. This earth itself is just a mud-pile whirling in infinite space. It is created for the time being so that the Jivas might carry on His play. When this play is over, it will be dissolved. Then man with a worldly wisdom laughs at others who quarrel over the objects of the senses. But the sage reminds him that, before gaining the knowledge of the impermanence of the objects, he, too, was behaving like the worldly men. With genuine love and sympathy, he makes people live in peace and gradually enlightens them about the real nature of the mundane objects and the Peace and the Bliss that can be had in the Self.

PARABLE OF THE MAN WHO PRETENDED TO BE A WOMAN AT THE BOOKING OFFICE

A man went to the railway station. He found that the Booking office was overcrowded and a long queue was waiting for the ticket. He wanted to get his ticket quickly. He looked around. He saw that a nearby window was absolutely free and there was no one taking a ticket at that window. He went over there. He found that it was for "Ladies Only." He was puzzled. A good man standing nearby understood the man's quest and said: "Cover your head with a veil and pretend that you are a woman. You can take the ticket." Without hesitating for a moment the man did so. He got the ticket. Another ticket examiner who was watching this, posted himself at the entrance to the platform and when the man reached that spot, he remarked: "But this is a Man's ticket!" The man with the veiled face, threw the cloth up and said: "Yes, yes; I am a man." All admired his intelligence.

All Jivas will eventually attain Moksha. But a wise one is eager to hasten the evolution and attain Moksha here and now. He is not willing to join the crowd. One in a million gets this urge. He looks around. He sees that while the Pravritti Marga is crowded with people and overcrowded with actions good and bad, which delay evolution, there is another—the Nivritti Marga—which does not have so much of a crowd. He goes there. But he finds that it is only for those who have certain qualifications. A sage, out of compassion for the aspirant, comes to his rescue and say: "You can go beyond the sex-idea if you forget that you are a man. You can conquer the inveterate foe, Abhimana, if you pretend you are a fool or a mad man. These are the secrets of this Path." The man implicitly obeys the sage. He gets wisdom of the Self. The foolish man of the world, vainly proud of his little intellect, mocks at the sage of wisdom, who behaves like a mad man. In an instant the saint throws away the veil of foolishness that he had purposely put on, and shines as a divine being among men, the Supreme, the God-man. He has attained his Goal. He gets easy entry into the Kingdom of Infinite Bliss.

PARABLE OF THE BULLOCK-CART DRIVER

A bullock-cart driver had discovered actually what Lord Brahma had destined for him. Brahma had willed at the birth of the bullock-cart driver that he would earn his living with the help of the bullock-cart. This had ensured that he would have two bullocks and a cart. When this truth dawned in him, the bullock-cart driver deviced a beautiful plan. He immediately sold away the bullocks and the cart and purchased all that was necessary for him and his family. He had saved nothing out of the sale proceeds. He returned home. He had nothing for the morrow. So, the Lord created a pair of bullocks and a cart and placed them in the man's empty shed. The bullock-cart driver, after a few days, sold them once again and distributed the amount in charity to the poor. Once again the Lord created the bullocks and the cart and placed them in the driver's shed.

Similar is the case with the sage of Self-realisation. He has discovered that his body is the result of his prarabdha and that whatever he is to get and to enjoy or suffer is predestined. He sees the workings of Karma very clearly. Therefore, he never bothers about the morrow. Whatever worldly possessions come to him, he at once distributes to others. He keeps nothing for himself. Naturally, in order to fulfil the Divine Will and to justify his prarabdha, the Lord grants him all the comforts and possessions once again. The Sage, too, goes on sharing his possessions with all the children of the Lord. He is free from anxiety and worry, because he knows that so long as the body lasts, what is predestined according to prarabdha will be granted. Thus he enjoys supreme peace and perfect contentment.

PARABLE OF THE PURANJANA MAHARAJA

In days of yore there was a king by name Puranjana. He had a friend known as Avijnata, the Unknown. The king parted company with this friend and wandered about seeking an abode. He rejected many kingdoms and arrived at a city which had nine gates and which was heavily guarded by five walls. In this city he met a beautiful lady surrounded by ten attendants and a five hooded serpent, that guarded her. Puranjana approached her and asked her to accept him. She, too, was happy beyond measure and married him and made him the ruler of her kingdom. There Puranjana ruled for a hundred years.

Puranjana went out daily through the nine gates of the city and brought back various objects and experiences. He was lost in sense-enjoyments and had so thoroughly identified himself with the queen that he seemed to have no individuality of his own.

One day Puranjana went out on a chariot of two wheels drawn by five horses. He killed many animals to satisfy his appetite for sense-enjoyments. On his return, though his wife was angry with him for thus abandoning her for a brief while, was soon pacified and once again she clasps the king in love. Thus Puranjana lived, without noticing the passage of time.

Old age assailed Puranjana. Chandavega, chief of the three-hundred and sixty-five Gandharvas (half of them fair and the others dark) repeatedly attacked Puranjana. But the great five-hooded serpent guarded the city. For full hundred years this battle raged and the serpent was successful in repelling the attack of Chandavega.

The daughter of Kala (Time), sought a husband; but no one accepted her. At last she approached Bhaya and wooed him, Bhaya offered her his army and also his brother Prajwara and induced her to destroy all beings. This army, accompanied by the daughter of Kala and Prajwara attacked Puranjana's city. Embraced by the daughter of Kala, the king underwent untold agony. When Prajagara's own home was attacked by the powerful army, this serpent was unable to withstand the onslaught and after a little struggle fled the city. In the meantime, Prajwara set the city ablaze. Though intensely attached to it, the king had to quit the city. Even at this moment, on account of his intense sense-craving, Puranjana was unable to remember his old friend Avijnata. While he was leaving the city, the animals which he had killed in the forest surrounded him and tortured him.

He was again born as the beautiful daughter of the king of Vidarbha. Maharaja Malayadhwaja married this princess. In due time, they got one daughter and seven sons. The Maharaja after entrusting the kingdom to his sons, went to the forest to meditate upon God. The Maharani, too, followed him. After intense penance, he obtained Darshan of the Lord; he entered into Samadhi and was oblivious of the surroundings. He realised his identity with the Supreme Brahman and was established in the Turiya State. When the Maharani discovered that only his body remained on earth, while his soul had attained union with the Supreme Soul, she prepared the husband's funeral and made up her mind to ascend the funeral pyre, to follow the husband. At that moment, her old friend the Avijnata appeared before her and reminded her that he was her friend birth after birth. He reminded her how, leaving him, she in her previous birth had gone over to the city of nine gates and underwent much suffering. He reveals that he and she are One and One alone. The soul of Vidarbhi awakened and attains union with the Supreme Brahman.

This parable illustrates the life of a Jiva here. Puranjana is the Jiva. Avijnata, the Unknown, is the Supreme Soul. After discarding many births as mineral, plant, animals, etc., the Jiva enters into the human body, the Navadwara-Puri. There are five Kosas that surround the Jiva here. The princess in this city is none other than intellect. The Jiva is wedded to the little human intellect. Residing in the body, it enjoys the pleasures of this world through ten various sense-avenues.

Riding the chariot of the body with its two wheels of good and evil, the Jiva performs many actions such as sacrificing animals in Yajnas, etc. The intellect gets reconciled to such actions and thus the Jiva and the intellect pass the time.

Chandavega represents the year, with its three hundred sixty-five days. Years attack the body; but the five-hooded serpent Prajagara (which is the five Mukhya-Pranas) repels all attacks and protects the city. But in due time old age overpowers the man.

At this time, a powerful army attacks him. It is the army which is led by Kala (Time or death), Bhaya (Great Fear) and Prajwara (mortal fever). The sensuous man who revelled in various objects of the senses now has to embrace cold and cruel death. The Prana is unable to face this new enemy. It departs. Mortal fever sets the body ablaze. Though unwilling, the Jiva has to quit the body. But on account of Moha, the Jiva is unable to recognise his kinship with the Great Unknown Being,

God. As he departs from this world, the various beings whom he harmed during his life here, pursue him and torture him.

Puranjana's rebirth as a girl is intended to show that the Jiva is beyond sex and takes as male or female in accordance with Karma. In this birth, however, the Jiva renounces all desires for sense-enjoyment, meditates on the Lord and eventually meets the Great Unknown Friend, God, who awakens the soul to its pristine glory. The Jiva realises its identity with the Supreme Being.

PARABLE OF THE UNWARY DEER

A deer was playing with its mate in a garden full of flowers. It was nibbling at grass. Its attention completely absorbed in the sweet humming of the bees, it failed to notice the hungry wolves approaching it, as also the hunter coming towards it with his arrow pointed at it. The hunter released the arrow and killed it in a minute, before it could realise its fate.

Similar is the case with a deluded man. His life on earth revolves round eating and procreation. Just as in the garden there are plenty of flowers, so also in the man's house there are beautiful women whose beauty lasts but for a short time and fades soon like the evening flower. The man, absorbed in the sweet talks of his wife and children, is oblivious of the wolves of years that are ready to devour his life. Here comes the hunter, Death, who, with one arrow, sends the man to the other world, before he could ever enquire into the nature of the Self.

O man, wake up and meditate on God. Waste not a single moment in sensual enjoyment.

PARABLE OF THE LACONIC SPARTAN

In the ancient Greece there was a tribe called Spartans. They were a very brave people, very simple in their habits, who never boasted about themselves. The valour of the Spartans was a legend all around their country. When a Spartan said that he would do something, people knew that he would rather die than fail to do that.

The place where they lived was called Laconia. So they were called Lacons. One of the injunctions of their ruler was: "Be brief, clear and accurate in what you say. Do not be vague, and do not waste unnecessary words in trying to say what you do not know. If you do not know a thing say so. If you want to do a thing, do not boast about it until you have accomplished it."

The people of Laconia were as obedient to their ruler as they were brave in the battle-field. In fact when asked a question, a Lacon's answer would be so brief and to the point that even to this day when a statement is succinct, it is called 'laconic.'

Now to illustrate the point, there is a story. In Northern Greece, King Philip, father of Alexander the Great, ruled over a territory called Macedonia. Philip wanted to conquer the entire Greece. So he raised an army of several legions and invaded many neighbouring states. Then he sent a note to the ruler of Spartans asking him to accept his sovereignty over Laconia. At the same time, he warned that if the Spartans failed to obey, his army would destroy them.

King Philip received the answer in a short while. The letter of the Spartan ruler contained only one word. The word was "If." It meant that the Spartans were not afraid of his army and that King Philip could carry out his threat only "if" his army was allowed to enter into Laconia by the gallant Lacons.

The world is full of vainglorious people. There is no dearth of gossipers. Practical people never indulge in boasting about their work.

They speak less and work more. They never promise or swear but do what is expected of them. They do not spread false rumours and fabricate facts. Talebearing is unknown to them. Vanity never clouds their reason. They avoid confusion by speaking less and by not listening to gossips. Hence their decisions are forthright and unswerving. The ancient people of Laconia present a fine example for emulation.

PARABLE OF MAHMUD AND AYAZ

Mahmud Gazni was a powerful emperor before whom the whole world trembled. But he was himself the deluded victim of the fascination of Ayaz, a slave-girl. He became so much infatuated with the love of Ayaz, that when she was near, he was powerless. Even when he attended the Court, his Prime Minister had to constantly remind him that he was the Mighty

Emperor Mahmud Gazni, the great conqueror, etc. Then and then alone was he able to behave as an emperor should.

Even so, the Jiva which is none other than the Infinite Consciousness, is deluded by Maya and comes to imagine that it is finite, powerless, feeble and limited, subject to birth and death, pain and joy, etc. The Prime Minister of the Jiva or the pure intellect tries to reflect deeply and raise the Vrittis of Akhanda, Ekarasa, Satchidananda, Nitya, Buddha, Mukta Swaroopa, etc., and the Sadhaka begins to meditate. During meditation the Jiva feels that it is one with the Infinite, unaffected by Maya and Avidya. Thus gradually it is established in this exalted state.

PARABLE OF THE DRAMATIC SHOW

The Principal of St. Joseph's academy organised a dramatic show entitled "Reunion." He announced that different actors would act on the stage for three hours and after the show, he would distribute prizes and cups, for good actors, in the presence of the distinguished gentry of the town. The very name of the drama fascinated me and I went to see it. Actors were given proper costumes and were told to act different roles. When everything was ready, the Principal declared the drama open and the drama commenced. A set of actors came, played their part and then disappeared. Another set of actors came and playing their part, too, disappeared likewise. The process was continuous. See that bad actor! He is not acting his role. He is retarding others in their acting. He is busy in correcting others in their acting. He is busy in correcting his costume, decorating his costume, but not doing his role. He thinks there is no Principal and the drama will never end and that he will continue to enjoy for ever and do as he likes. He is a fool though he thinks he is wise. The Principal and the gentry have spotted him. He is spoiling the whole show. The Principal is very forgiving and so he did not remove him from the stage at once, but waited till his part was over, and then he was punished for his misdeeds and was weeping.

Here comes a good actor. His acting is fine. He had acute backache; but he now seems to have entirely forgotten all about that ache of his and is busy acting his role as best as he could, he is lost in it. He firmly believes that the show will end after but three hours and then the Principal will adjudge all the actors. His only concern is to play now his role to the best of his powers. He did play his role in a fine manner and now all are praising him for the way he acted. He has won the hearts of all the spectators.

Soon the show was over. All those actors that were selected for awards were escorted with honour to the dais. The Principal and the gentry were visibly pleased with them. They were all called out one after the other and were awarded their allotted prizes, cups and various other honours; and they were in great joy. It was a grand show, this one. While returning home, I was caught in a reverie, going over the whole show of the evening once again mentally and murmuring to myself.

OTHER PARABLES

God has organised a similar dramatic show of this world entitled 'God-realisation'. He has announced through prophets and saints that Jivatmas will act for a definite number of years, wearing different bodies. The breaths of all bodies are counted. Then He will judge all and give cups and prizes of eternity to good actors in the presence of saints of divine court. God gave bodies to Jivatmas and assigned different roles to them. When He created the world this world-drama started. A set of bodies come, play their part and then disappear. Another set of actors come and disappear likewise. The process is continuous. See that bad actor. He is not acting his role and is retarding others in doing Bhakti. He is attached to his body and is ever busy in feeding it and maintaining it and in enjoying worldly pleasures and not doing Bhakti to God. He thinks there is no God; he will never cast off his body, but will continue to enjoy body pleasures for ever as he likes. He is a fool though he thinks he is wise. God and His courtiers are watching him all the time. He is a blot on the world-drama. God is very forgiving and does not punish him at once. He waits till he finishes his part and then He punishes him and he weeps.

Here comes a good person. He lives the divine life. He may have a diseased body, but he has forgotten all about the diseased condition of his body. He is ever busy doing Bhakti to God with all his power. He firmly believes that he must die sometime and that God will judge all. His only worry is to do Bhakti as much as he can. He has won the hearts of all and all praise him now. When he casts away his body, he is escorted to the

Court of God with honours. God and His courtiers are pleased to see Bhaktas. God calls them one after the other and awards the prizes and cups of eternity and then they are in great joy and bliss.

Let us become good actors in this world-drama. Forget worrying about disease and death. They are sure to come. Adapt to circumstances and keep busy in Bhakti. Food, dress, and worldly actions are necessary, but above all is Bhakti of God, which is the role for which God has given this body. Let us do it even now and deserve God's praises and honours in the Court of the Divine, and enjoy Bliss Infinite.

THE DIVINE LIFE SOCIETY

The Divine Life Society was founded by His Holiness Sri Swami Sivanandaji Maharaj in the year 1936, for the widest possible propagation of the most precious and the best elements of the great Culture and living Idealism of Inner India. His Holiness strove ceaselessly through this Society and the Ashram to bring about a world-wide dissemination of the vital, ethical and spiritual ideal of India and to broadcast the knowledge of Yoga, Vedanta, Dharma and an exemplary life of divine virtues, right conduct, selfless service, universal brotherhood and the unity of life as a whole.

The Headquarters of this Society are housed at Shivanandanagar, on the right bank of the Ganga, in Rishikesh, at the foothills of the Himalayas. Here labour a band of Sannyasins and Sadhakas, whose lives are entirely dedicated to the service of humanity, to learn and put into practice the Yoga of Synthesis and to function actively as dynamic centres of spirituality. The Society has as its aim the awakening of humanity to the true and lofty purpose of life, enlightening them on the various means and methods of attaining the Goal of life, and inspiring them and urging them to strive for its attainment.

The Divine Life Society carries out its object of a world-wide revival of spirituality through publication of books, pamphlets and magazines dealing scientifically with all the aspects of Yoga and Vedanta, universal religion and philosophy, and ancient medicine; holding and arranging cultural and spiritual conferences and discourses; establishing training centres for the practice of Yoga and the revival of true culture; and taking such other steps from time to time as may be necessary for bringing about a quick moral and spiritual regeneration in the world.

This Institution serves as a place of preservation of the ancient traditions and cultural practices that have come down as a time-honoured heritage. It has been built up to serve as a model of many-sided, altruistic activity, an ideal to copy, intended to bring about a complete unfoldment of the human personality, and to reveal the essential blending together of all sides of human nature. The Society also functions as an ideal place of retreat for the educated citizen of the world, wherein he can renew himself and recreate and refresh his being physically, mentally, morally and spiritually.

DEPARTMENTS OF SERVICE

The following are some of the important Departments of The Divine Life Society:

The Yoga-Vedanta Forest Academy, which trains seekers in the knowledge and practice of Yoga in its various aspects; *The Yoga-Vedanta Forest Academy Press,* which prints the spiritual Books, Journals and other literature of the Society; *The Sivananda Publication League,* which caters to the public these valuable publications; *The Free Literature Section,* which distributes freely literature worth several thousands of rupees, every year; *The Annapurna Annakshetra,* which is the common kitchen of the Ashram; *The Guest-House,* which looks to the needs of the many visitors and guests who come to the Ashram for spiritual guidance and training; *The Temples* of worship, which hold prayers for the peace of the world and conduct regular Sankirtan of the Divine Name for commonweal; the two monthly *Journals* ('*The Divine Life*' in English and '*Divya Jivan*' in Hindi), which publish essays and articles on sublime philosophy and provide guidance of topical value to all the seekers and students of Yoga; *The Library,* which provides reading of some of the most precious books on philosophy, Religion and Yoga, etc.; *The Correspondence Section,* which furnishes proper replies to countless queries that come from seekers all over the world in the various fields of life; *The Social Service Wing,* which attends to such services as Leprosy Relief, Medical Aid to the poor and needy, Education of poor students even up to a high standard of qualification; providing relief both in cash and in kind to destitutes and the disabled, wherever necessary; and cultural and spiritual tours and conferences by the president of the Society for the benefit of the aspiring souls in the different parts of the country and abroad. The Society has a large number of *Branches,* functioning in India as well as the other countries in the world.

The Daily Programme of the Ashram at the Headquarters includes Group Prayers and Meditation; Worship; Practice of Yoga Exercises; Discourses on Yoga,

Vedanta and the Bhagavadgita; regular Meditation Session; and General Satsanga; in addition to the Services rendered through the Departments of Activity mentioned above.

These services and activities of the Ashram are so conceived and conducted that they form a vehicle for the expression of the spiritual aspirations of seekers and become a venue for manifesting in practical life the broad-based spiritual ideal of the Oneness of God, the brotherhood of creation and the immortality of the soul.

The fundamental aims and objects of the Divine Life Society, as a whole, are purely spiritual, entirely non-sectarian, universally applicable and perfectly tolerant. The Society offers a peaceful haven wherein is provided ample opportunity and actual help for the restoration of peace to the troubled, conflict-ridden and psychologically traumatised personality of the modern man. The Aim is Life in the Universal Divine Being; to reconcile the outward activities and functions of human society, as well as the inner aspirations of the human individual with the universal demands of the Cosmic Nature and of the Absolute.